TOPICS TODAY

W9-CLJ-349

Protecting Civil Liberties

By Sadie Silva

Cavendish
Square

New York

Published in 2022 by Cavendish Square Publishing, LLC
29 E. 21st Street New York, NY 10010

Copyright © 2022 by Cavendish Square Publishing, LLC

First Edition

Portions of this work were originally authored by Leanne Currie-McGhee and published as *Civil Liberties (Hot Topics)*. All new material this edition authored by Sadie Silva.

All websites were available and accurate when this book was sent to press.

Library of Congress Cataloging-in-Publication Data

Names: Silva, Sadie, author.
Title: Protecting civil liberties / Sadie Silva.
Description: New York : Cavendish Square Publishing, [2022] | Series: Topics today | Includes bibliographical references and index.
Identifiers: LCCN 2021005469 | ISBN 9781502661050 (library binding) | ISBN 9781502661043 (paperback) | ISBN 9781502661067 (ebook)
Subjects: LCSH: Civil rights–United States.
Classification: LCC KF4749 .S557 2022 | DDC 342.7308/5–dc23
LC record available at https://lccn.loc.gov/2021005469

Editor: Caitie McAneney
Copyeditor: Nicole Horning
Designer: Deanna Paternostro

Some of the images in this book illustrate individuals who are models. The depictions do not imply actual situations or events.

CPSIA compliance information: Batch #CS22CSQ: For further information contact Cavendish Square Publishing LLC, New York, New York, at 1-877-980-4450.

Printed in the United States of America

Find us on

CONTENTS

Edwardus
dei gratia
rex Angl
dominus
hibnie et
dux aq
tannie
Archieps
epis Abbi
bus prioribus Comitibus Baronibus
Justic vicecomitibus prepositis mi
nistris et omnibus ballivis et fide
libus suis salutem. Inspeximus
magnam cartam dni H quonda
regis Anglie epis nostri de liberta
tibus Anglie in hec verba. Henr
nus dei gratia rex Anglie dns
hibnie et dux et comes Norman et Aquit
tannie et Comes Andegavie. Ar
chiepis Epis Abbatibus prioribus Co
mitibus Baronibus vicecomitibus
prepositis ministris et omnibus
ballivis et fidelibus suis presentem
cartam inspecturis salutem. Sciat
tis quod nos intuitu dei et pro salu
te anime nostre et omnium antecess
sorum et successorum nostrorum ad ex
altacionem sancte ecclesie et emen
dacionem regni nostri spontanea et
bona voluntate nostra dedimus
et concessimus Archiepis epis
Abbatibus prioribus comitibus baro
nibus et omnibus de regno nostro has
libertates subscriptas tenendas in
regno nostro Anglie imperpetuum. In
primis concessimus deo et hac

presenti carta nostra confirmavimus
pro nobis et heredibus nostris imperpe
tuum ecclesia Anglicana libera sit et habeat
omnia iura sua integra et libertates
suas illesas. Concessimus etiam
et dedimus omnibus liberis hominibus
regni nostri pro nobis et heredibus nostris
imperpetuum has libertates subscripta
habend et tenend eis et heredibus suis
de nobis et heredibus nostris imperpetuum.
Si quis comitum vel baro
num nostrorum sive aliorum tenencium
de nobis in capite per servicium
militare mortuus fuerit et cum
decesserit heres eius plene etatis
fuerit et relevium debeat habeat here
ditatem suam per antiquum relevi
um scilicet heres vel heredes
comitis de comitatu integro per cen
tum libras heres vel heredes
baronis de baronia integra per
centum marcas heres vel heredes
militis de feodo militis integro
per centum solidos ad plus et
qui minus fuerit minus det
secundum antiquam consuetudinem
feodorum. Si autem heres a
licuius talium infra etatem fuerit
dominus eius non habeat custodiam
eius nec terre sue antequam ho
magium eius ceperit. Et post
quam talis heres fuerit in custo
dia cum ad etatem pervenerit
scilicet viginti unius annorum
habeat hereditatem suam sine re
levio et sine fine. Ita tamen

THE VALUE OF CIVIL LIBERTIES

In 1940, President Franklin Delano Roosevelt said, "We must scrupulously guard the civil rights and civil liberties of all our citizens, whatever their background. We must remember that any oppression, any injustice, any hatred, is a wedge designed to attack our civilization."[1] Civil liberties are the backbone of fair government. These rights, which we might sometimes take for granted, are not guaranteed for everyone. People risked their lives for hundreds of years in the fight against oppressive systems to gain basic rights. In some parts of the world, people are still fighting for the civil liberties that we enjoy in the United States, and in the United States, not all Americans are treated equally even today.

Some of the first guaranteed civil liberties were achieved through the Magna Carta. English nobles forced King John to sign this historic document in 1215, which ensured that the king of England would respect the rights of his subjects. One of the rights was habeas corpus, which allowed the king's subjects to appeal against unlawful imprisonment. The Magna Carta was a founding document of democracy, which shaped the way the U.S. Founding Fathers set up the limitations of the United States government.

◀ The Magna Carta was one of the inspirations behind the U.S. Constitution and one of the first documents to guarantee civil liberties to a group of citizens.

The philosophy of natural rights is often attributed to Enlightenment thinkers in the 17th century. Enlightenment philosopher John Locke published *Two Treatises of Government* in 1689, which declared that all people are born with natural rights. He wrote:

> *The state of nature has a law of nature to govern it, which obliges every one: and reason, which is that law, teaches all mankind, who will but consult it, that being all equal and independent, no one ought to harm another in his life, health, liberty, or possessions.*[2]

These Enlightenment ideas sparked movements across the world over the following centuries, most famously in the American colonies in the 18th century. In 1775, the American Revolution began between England and its American colonies. As the new United States set about creating their founding documents, they called upon the ideas in the Magna Carta and from Enlightenment thinkers. The framers of government included a Bill of Rights as an addition to the U.S. Constitution to specifically protect certain liberties for citizens.

Civil liberties have continued to be a core value of the United States. Americans value their rights to freedom of speech, freedom of the press, and freedom of religion, among others. There have been violations of civil liberties since the United States was founded, especially for minorities and marginalized communities. However, the U.S. Constitution allows for amendments, or changes; thus, throughout its history, people have called on the U.S. government to change laws around civil liberties to make the United States fairer for all. This is generally done through a system of voting for desired elected officials and public protest and demonstration. In the United States, people are free to protest the government as long as they follow certain rules. They can make speeches and signs, march, and speak their beliefs. If many people march at once, it can bring national attention to their issue, which happened during the Women's March in 2017, which called attention to women's rights.

What happens if the constitutionality of civil liberties is called into question? That's a matter for the courts. The U.S. federal court system often hears cases that involve the infringement, or violation,

On January 21, 2017, as many as 4.6 million people attended events across the United States connected with the Women's March for gender equality and civil rights. Many believed it was the largest single-day demonstration in U.S. history.

of civil liberties. There are different levels to this court system. Cases are generally first heard in the lower courts; however, if they are appealed, they may head to a higher court. The highest court in the United States is the Supreme Court. When a case is ruled on in the Supreme Court, it sets a precedent, or rule, for the whole country. The Supreme Court chooses cases that concern important questions about federal laws and the U.S. Constitution. Their rulings have a huge impact on the country. For example, in 1954, the Supreme Court ruled that segregated schools are inherently unequal, which led to integration of Black and white schools. In 2020, the Supreme Court ruled that federal civil rights laws protect LGBTQ+ employees from workplace discrimination nationwide.

While the United States guarantees rights to its citizens, many other countries do not. Some countries, such as the United Kingdom, New Zealand, and Israel, don't specifically guarantee all the liberties Americans have or don't have one official written constitution. Saudi Arabia operates on sharia law, which is derived from a strict interpretation, or understanding, of Islam. China has a constitution that guarantees civil liberties for its citizens, but the government suppresses, or puts down, opposition to its policies. People who speak out against the Chinese government may be arrested. This was made worse during the presidency of Xi Jinping, who took office in 2013. Journalists have been held in Chinese prisons for criticizing the government. In July 2020, the Chinese government passed the National Security Law, which was aimed at stopping opposition to the Communist Party in Hong Kong. This

Christians gathered in Hong Kong in 2019 as part of a pro-democracy peaceful protest.

allowed China to suppress the civil liberties of people in Hong Kong, and experts feared it would lead to human rights abuses.

Citizens in the United States and around the world are passionate about protecting their civil liberties. Organizations like the American Civil Liberties Union (ACLU) and the United Nations (UN) investigate civil rights violations and human rights abuses. They try to hold governments accountable when they fail to protect their citizens' rights. Of course, the issues of civil liberties are often complicated, and some cases are not clear. For example, in some cases, people's rights are put aside in favor of national security or safety. In complicated cases, courts, lawmakers, leaders, advocacy groups, and citizens work together to find a solution. These fights for civil liberties can sometimes get heated; however, from such fights, people have gained rights to marry who they choose, go to the schools they choose, attend the place of worship they choose, and more.

CIVIL LIBERTIES AND THE AMERICAN STORY

America was founded upon a call for liberty. It was one of the main considerations of the Founding Fathers as they sought to break from England. England's actions of discounting civil liberties and imposing unfair taxes and regulations on its colonies sparked a revolution.

The word liberty is woven into the foundational documents of the American republic. Within the preamble to the U.S. Constitution, the Founding Fathers pledged to "secure the blessings of liberty."[1] The words within the Declaration of Independence and U.S. Constitution are still used today to justify the importance of civil liberties in American society.

The American Revolution

England's first permanent settlement in North America was Jamestown, founded in 1607. From the beginning, the colonies practiced limited forms of self-government. England was an ocean away, so each colony made its own colonial legislatures. Many people also fled England to escape religious persecution, so the ability to practice their religion was an incredibly important right for them.

After the French and Indian War (1754–1763), which was fought in North America, England had a lot of debt. The British government decided to impose new taxes on its American

◀ Following the passage of the Stamp Act, which put a tax on newspapers and certain documents in the American colonies, the colonists protested—sometimes violently, as shown here.

colonists. Many of these taxes, such as those that followed the passage of the Sugar Act and Stamp Act, were seen as wildly unfair.

The British also cracked down on colonial smuggling, forcing colonists to buy goods only from England. The Townshend Acts, passed in 1767, were a British attempt to exert authority over the colonies. This led to protests and boycotts, which prompted England to send British soldiers to Boston, Massachusetts. Tensions rose with events such as the Boston Massacre (1770) and Boston Tea Party (1773). They reached a boiling point when England imposed the Intolerable Acts (also called the Coercive Acts) in 1774, which, among other unjust policies, forced colonists to house British soldiers. This was the final straw for some colonists, who decided to meet as the First Continental Congress. The following year, the Founding Fathers met again, as the Second Continental Congress, to list their grievances to England and, eventually, declare independence.

The Founding Fathers wrote the Declaration of Independence in 1776. They explained why America broke from Great Britain. According to the Declaration of Independence, people have natural rights that should not be abused by the government:

> *We hold these truths to be self-evident, that all men are created equal, that they are endowed by their Creator with certain unalienable Rights, that among these are Life, Liberty and the pursuit of Happiness.—That to secure these rights, Governments are instituted among Men, deriving their just powers from the consent of the governed.*[2]

This document said something revolutionary for that time: The

During the Boston Massacre, a mob of angry colonists confronted British soldiers in Boston. The soldiers killed five colonists, which sparked fury in the colonies.

power of government comes from the people. "Liberty" was a rallying cry throughout the bloody years of revolution. This was illustrated in 1775 when Founding Father Patrick Henry gave a famous speech to the Second Virginia Convention in which he said, "Give me liberty, or give me death!"[3]

Americans won the war for their independence in 1783. After the war, the U.S. Constitution and the Bill of Rights were written and approved. These documents set up how the United States governs and how it protects citizens' liberties to this day.

Our Defining Document

The Declaration of Independence expressed the Founding Fathers' intent to become independent from England and to establish a new country rooted in liberty for its citizens. Then came the challenge of winning a war and setting up a whole new government. The first constitution, the Articles of Confederation, failed because states were afraid to have a strong federal government. They wanted the freedom to do what was best for *their* people. At what's become known as the Constitutional Convention, leaders had a huge task—to create a new constitution that gave enough power to the federal government for it to be effective, while balancing power with the state governments. They also aimed to prevent any one branch of government from gaining too much power.

Some Founding Fathers, such as James Madison, worried that a strong national government could violate citizens' freedoms, just as the British government had. "The essence of Government is power; and power, lodged as it must be in human hands, will ever be liable to abuse,"[4] Madison wrote. He wanted to add a bill of rights to the Constitution to protect people's freedoms from government abuse.

The U.S. Constitution was written in 1787, was ratified in 1788, and has been in operation since 1789. It is the framework of

The U.S. Constitution starts with "We the people." This indicated that the power in the United States should rest with the people.

The Bill of Rights

The Bill of Rights lists specific freedoms that the U.S. government cannot take away from people. They are the first 10 amendments, or changes, to the Constitution. The First Amendment is often regarded as the most important; it ensures the freedom of speech, freedom of the press, and the right of the people "peaceably to assemble, and to petition the Government for a redress of grievances."[1] Many people who support gun rights in the United States care a lot about the Second Amendment, which gives people the right to keep and bear arms.

The Bill of Rights also restricts what the government can do to people, which is a direct reflection of how the British government had abused its colonists. For example, the Third Amendment protects against quartering, or forcing people to house soldiers without their consent.

The Bill of Rights further protects people's privacy by restricting the government's ability to conduct unreasonable searches and seizures of people and their property. It prohibits the government from establishing a national religion. It does not allow the government to deprive any person of life, liberty, or property without due process of law. The Bill of Rights also protects those accused of crimes by guaranteeing people a speedy public trial by an unbiased jury.

The Bill of Rights sets the United States apart from other countries that don't guarantee these freedoms. People often point to these amendments as precedents for how they should be treated when they feel their liberties have been threatened.

1. Quoted in Thomas Greenleaf and James Madison Pamphlet Collection, "The conventions of a number of the states having, at the time of their adopting the Constitution, expressed a desire, in order to prevent misconstruction or abuse of its powers, that further declaratory and restrictive clauses should be added ... Resolved, by the Senate and House of Representatives ... that the following articles be proposed to the legislatures of the several states, as amendments to the Constitution," 1789, www.loc.gov/item/92838253/.

the U.S. government, setting up the three branches of government and explaining how they work together. Later, the Bill of Rights was added and became an essential part of the document, as it promises the basic civil liberties that Americans hold as part of their identity.

Liberty for All

The U.S. Pledge of Allegiance declares that the nation provides "liberty and justice for all."[5] The U.S. Constitution and Bill of Rights, state constitutions, and all laws apply to anyone within the country unless stated otherwise in the law itself. According to *Slate* magazine, "the Bill of Rights applies to everyone, even *illegal* immigrants. So an immigrant, legal or illegal, prosecuted under the criminal code has the right to due process, a speedy and public trial, and other rights protected by the Fifth and Sixth Amendments."[6]

The scope of the Bill of Rights wasn't always so wide. When it was first created, the Bill of Rights applied only to the federal government. That meant that state and local governments could still make laws that violated the Bill of Rights and citizens' civil liberties. In 1833, the Supreme Court specifically ruled in the case of *Barron v. Baltimore* that the Bill of Rights applied only to the federal government.

This changed when the 14th Amendment was added to the Constitution following the American Civil War (1861–1865). It was one of three amendments added to secure the rights of those who had formerly been enslaved. The 14th Amendment defines citizenship and guarantees that formerly enslaved people are U.S. citizens and, as such, must have their rights protected by the states. It also guarantees due process and equal protection under the law. The Supreme Court has interpreted this amendment to mean that state governments must follow the Bill of Rights and not deny basic rights to any citizens.

Denying Civil Rights

While the Declaration of Independence famously declares the equality of all people, the history of the United States shows many instances in which the nation denied rights to different individuals and groups. For example, until 1865, many Black people were enslaved in America. According to the American Civil Liberties Union (ACLU):

> *Slavery was this country's original sin. For the first 78 years after it was ratified, the Constitution protected slavery and legalized racial subordination. Instead of constitutional rights, slaves were governed by "slave codes" that controlled every aspect of their lives. They had no access to the rule of law: they could not go to court, make*

contracts, or own any property. They could be whipped, branded, imprisoned without trial, and hanged.[7]

The Civil War resulted in the abolishment of slavery. Amendments were then added to the Constitution to protect the liberties of former slaves. The 13th Amendment officially put an end to slavery. The 14th Amendment guaranteed Black Americans the right to due process and granted them citizenship. The 15th Amendment prevented the government from denying a person the right to vote because of their race.

Despite these changes, civil rights abuses continued. "Separate but equal" was a phrase used to describe segregation. Black people and white people had separate schools, restaurants, and other facilities. The Supreme Court heard the case of *Plessy v. Ferguson* in 1896. This case concerned the segregation on railroad cars. The Supreme Court upheld that separate but equal public facilities did not violate the Constitution. The Court, however, did not acknowledge that the separate facilities were not really equal, as white facilities were far superior in most cases.

Native Americans, immigrants, women, and LGBTQ+ Americans have also faced unequal conditions and rights in the United States throughout its history. The ACLU stated, "The most common constitutional violations went unchallenged because the people whose rights were most often denied were precisely those members of society who

---

Civil Liberties Amendments to the U.S. Constitution

1791: The first 10 amendments to the Constitution are ratified, called the Bill of Rights.

1865: The 13th Amendment passes, abolishing slavery.

1868: The 14th Amendment passes, extending citizenship to all Americans born or naturalized in the United States.

1870: The 15th Amendment outlaws the denial of the right to vote based on race, color, or previous servitude. However, discriminatory practices were adopted in many places to keep Black Americans from voting until 1965.

1920: The 19th Amendment gives women the right to vote.

Justice and Change

How can people challenge constitutional violations of civil rights? One way is through the justice system. Over its history, the U.S. Supreme Court has ruled to change some unfair laws and practices. The 20th century saw great progress in overturning old norms and creating more constitutional safeguards for the civil rights of minority groups. For example, the Supreme Court reversed its separate-but-equal ruling in 1954. In *Brown v. Board of Education of Topeka*, the Court ruled that it was unconstitutional to create separate schools because of race.

Following that case, the Supreme Court upheld federal laws that barred discrimination in other areas, such as public transportation. The Court also ruled that a state law against interracial marriage was invalid. From this point on, the government protected more of the civil liberties of Black Americans. However, even today, the fight for the protection of Black Americans' natural rights continues.

It may seem as if the power for change rests with only a handful of appointed officials. However, much progress has been made in the United States through nonviolent demonstrations and protests. The civil rights movement of the 1950s and 1960s brought international attention to the injustices faced by Black Americans. Movements by Latinx people, LGBTQ+ people, Native Americans, Americans with disabilities, and women have also been successful in pushing for new legislation and leading to new precedents and civil liberty safeguards.

were least aware of their rights and least able to afford a lawyer. They had no access to those impenetrable bulwarks of liberty – the courts. The Bill of Rights was like an engine no one knew how to start."[8]

Fighting for Civil Liberties

Organizations exist in the United States and around the world to protect civil and human rights. The United Nations (UN) works to protect people's natural rights on a global level. In 1948, the UN issued the Universal Declaration of Human Rights, which states, "Everyone is entitled to all the rights and freedoms set forth in this Declaration,

In 1948, the United Nations passed the Universal Declaration of Human Rights as an international common standard of fundamental, or basic, human rights.

without distinction of any kind, such as race, color, sex, language, religion, political or other opinion, national or social origin, property, birth or other status."[9]

The declaration outlines 30 rights the UN believes all people have, such as free speech. It also includes the right to a life of security. According to this document, people should not have to endure torture and violence. They should be able to live where they want to and not be restricted, meaning that governments should not regulate where a person can live. They should have the freedom to move to a different city or even a different country if they choose. The UN's goal is to get all countries to protect these rights. In 1948, 48 countries, including the United States, voted in favor of this resolution. The organization's hope is that more governments around the world will continue to recognize and protect people's inherent rights.

One of the most important civil liberties organizations in America is the ACLU. One of the organization's first cases was about freedom of speech and freedom of religion, called *Tennessee v. John Scopes.*

In 1943, the ACLU won a religious freedom case. At the time, public schools required all students to salute the U.S. flag. Jehovah's Witnesses did not want their children to salute the flag because they view it as worshipping an object. The ACLU argued that the requirement to salute the flag violated religious freedom. In the case, *West Virginia State Board of Education v. Barnette,* the Supreme Court ruled that Jehovah's

Roger Baldwin founded the ACLU in 1920.

Tennessee v. John Scopes

ACLU attorney Clarence Darrow defended John Scopes in *Tennessee v. John Scopes* in 1925. Scopes was a teacher who taught the theory of evolution in his class. This violated a state law that did not allow public schoolteachers to teach evolution theory. The law was in place because the evolution theory contradicted the biblical account of the world's creation. The ACLU claimed that the law violated religious freedom because the government, which runs the public schools, was supporting a religious belief. The law did not keep church and state issues separate. The ACLU said the Tennessee law also violated the freedom of speech by not allowing teachers to freely speak.

At the time, evolution was a controversial issue. Creationism was taught in many schools despite its religious basis, and it was supported by many people. Public rallies against the ACLU and its defense filled the streets in front of the courthouse. The judge, John Raulston, was a deeply religious man. He started the trial with a prayer and quoted scripture at different times throughout the proceedings. He also did not allow certain scientific testimony in support of evolution. The ACLU did not win the case, and Scopes was convicted. The trial, however, was famous, so it brought attention to the ACLU and to civil liberty issues.

Witnesses could refuse to salute the flag.

In recent years, the ACLU has won cases to help LGBTQ+ Americans openly serve in the military, protect reproductive rights, and allow same-sex couples to marry. Today, it continues to be one of America's most prominent civil liberties organizations.

Your Opinion Matters!

1. How did British treatment of American colonists affect how the Founding Fathers approached writing the U.S. Constitution?

2. Why do you think the concept of "liberty" is so important in the United States?

3. Why is it important to protest for civil liberties even today?

THE IMPORTANCE OF FREE SPEECH

Freedom of speech allows people to express their opinions for or against government actions, which isn't possible in some other countries. This constitutional promise protects people who seek political change by criticizing the government and its policies. This is important because if the First Amendment did not exist in the United States, the government would be able to arrest anyone who said something it objected to. People would be afraid to speak up, and social problems would never be solved. "The beauty of free speech is that it serves as the ultimate protection of minority viewpoints, ensuring that no matter the political tide, all people will be allowed to speak their minds,"[1] wrote Robert Shibley, executive director of the Foundation for Individual Rights in Education (FIRE).

While freedom of speech is one of America's most treasured liberties, it is sometimes misunderstood. The Bill of Rights protects Americans from being punished by the government for speaking their minds as long as they are not encouraging criminal activity, threatening others, or lying about people to get them in trouble. However, harmful speech still may have consequences, even if it isn't seen as criminal. Saying things that are racist, sexist, or otherwise objectionable may cause someone to lose their job or professional connections. If someone spreads disinformation (false and deliberately misleading statements) or threats online, they may have their social media accounts reported or removed. This is not a violation of free speech because private organizations are allowed

◀ Speaking out against government actions is a hallmark of American civil liberties.

to decide who they want to be associated with. Similarly, if a publication prints something many people dislike, it is not a violation of free speech or a free press for people to cancel their subscriptions or for advertisers to stop supporting the publication. Freedom of speech is one of the foundational values of American democracy, and it's often at the forefront of political debates over civil liberties.

Restricted Speech Around the World

People in the United States are guaranteed the right to free speech, but this isn't true everywhere in the world. In some countries, people are restricted in what they can say or write. Typically, governments restrict free speech because government leaders do not want to be questioned. They want to rule their way, with no criticism or opposition. Journalists can be jailed for writing against the government. In 2019, journalist Kate Hodal wrote in *The Guardian*, "Nearly half the world's people are living in countries where their freedom of speech and right to privacy are being eroded … 'Strongman' regimes seeking to squash voices of dissent and solidify political power are increasingly monitoring citizens through technology, cracking down on protests and jailing journalists."[2] Countries with increasing restrictions on speech and press included Turkey, Cambodia, Kenya, Kyrgyzstan, and Venezuela, among others.

Iran is another country that restricts free expression. The Iranian government restricts reporters and visitors from other nations. Visitors can be jailed for questioning or criticizing the government. In 2015, Jason Rezaian, who held dual citizenship in Iran and the United States, was serving as a reporter for the *Washington Post* when he was arrested in Iran. Rezaian spent 544 days in jail on unspecified charges. The Iranian government denied him the right to meet with his lawyer or understand the charges against him. With the help of the United States, Rezaian was released in January 2016.

China's constitution states, "Citizens of the People's Republic of China enjoy freedom of speech, of the press, of assembly, of association, of procession and of demonstratiion."[3] However, China is one of the most restrictive countries in the world when it comes to freedom of expression and privacy. The government does not allow citizens to openly criticize its policies. Discussion of controversial subjects is restricted on the internet in China. In 2020, China rolled out a "social credit system," which seeks to give citizens a social credit score based on their social, political, and economic behavior. Mass surveillance and artificial intelligence programs are used to keep track of peoples' behavior, which may be incredibly dangerous in China and in the wider world when it comes to civil liberties.

Limits to Free Speech in America

Even in the United States, there are limits to free speech. The freedom of speech is a fundamental right, but it is not absolute. For example, people cannot use speech to incite violence or make a direct threat against a person or group.

In the United States, people are restricted from saying "fighting words"—words that are meant to inflict injury and incite violence—to another person. This restriction came from a New Hampshire court case that made it to the Supreme Court. A New Hampshire court convicted a man for making offensive comments to a city official. He violated a state law that did not allow people to use insulting language toward people in public places. In 1942, the Supreme Court heard his case, *Chaplinsky v. New Hampshire*. The Court upheld the state's decision to convict Chaplinsky. According to the majority opinion, "There are certain well-defined and narrowly limited classes of speech, the prevention and punishment of which have never been thought to raise any constitutional problem. These include … 'fighting' words—those which by their very utterance inflict injury or tend to incite an immediate breach of the peace."[4]

It is not always easy to determine what can be considered fighting words. For example, some people believe that all hate speech should be considered fighting words. Hate speech refers to words meant to attack a person or group of people based on their race, religion, nationality, or other factors. Other people don't consider hate speech fighting words. According to these people, hate speech may be offensive, but if it doesn't directly cause violence or illegal actions, then it's still protected by the Constitution.

Many college campuses have codes that restrict hate speech. People who agree with these hate speech codes say that the harm the codes prevent is more important than the freedoms they limit. People who are targeted by hate speech are often from marginalized communities, and they deserve to attend school without feeling threatened or discriminated against. Those who criticize hate speech codes say that some students with unpopular

Inciting Insurrection

January 6, 2021, was one of the darkest days in the United States since the American Civil War. Congress was set to meet to certify the results of the 2020 presidential election, in which former-Vice President Joseph R. Biden Jr. won against incumbent (current office holder) President Donald J. Trump. That day, just before Congress began their ceremonial proceedings, Trump spoke at a "Save America" rally. Participants denied the results of the objectively free and fair election, which Trump falsely claimed was "stolen" from him. For months, he and some his supporters had spread a campaign of disinformation online that claimed the election was stolen. Spreading disinformation is not a crime in the United States. However, soon, Trump and some allies did breach the limits of free speech when they incited an insurrection at the Save America rally.

At the rally, Trump's personal lawyer, Rudy Giuliani, said, "Let's have trial by combat."[1] Trump said, "And we fight. We fight ... and if you don't fight ... you're not going to have a country anymore."[2] He encouraged the group to march down Pennsylvania Avenue to the U.S. Capitol, where Congress was meeting, promising to join them (which he never did). He said, "You'll never take back our country with weakness. You have to show strength, and you have to be strong."[3] In the hours that followed, the riotous mob took Trump's words seriously. They descended upon the U.S. Capitol, breaking past barricades and eventually entering the building. Armed with

opinions may feel threatened by "politically correct" students, which may harm social institutions.

Civil liberties organizations such as the ACLU fight against hate speech codes. They believe all speech, even hate speech, is protected by the Bill of Rights and that if one group is silenced, it is possible for the government to justify silencing other groups. The ACLU argues that if hate speech is allowed, people can debate it and come to their own opinion about it:

> Where racist, sexist and homophobic speech is concerned, the ACLU believes that more speech—not less—is the best revenge. This is particularly true at universities, whose mission is to facilitate learning through open debate and study, and to enlighten. Speech codes are not the way to go on campuses, where all views are entitled to be heard, explored, supported or refuted. Besides, when hate is out in the open, people can see the

guns and restraint devices, they sought to harm Congress members and Vice President Mike Pence. The group defaced the building, stole classified information and government property, and terrorized government officials, journalists, and Capitol staff through threats and violence. At least five people died that day at the event. While Trump said his words had been appropriate, the House of Representatives impeached him for incitement just a week later, claiming that his words led directly to the insurrection at the U.S. Capitol.

1. Quoted in "Rudy Giuliani Speech Transcript at Trump's Washington, D.C. Rally: Wants 'Trial by Combat,'" The Rev, January 6, 2021, www.rev.com/blog/transcripts/rudy-giuliani-speech-transcript-at-trumps-washington-d-c-rally-wants-trial-by-combat.

2. Quoted in "Donald Trump Speech 'Save America' Rally Transcript January 6," The Rev, January 6, 2021, www.rev.com/blog/transcripts/donald-trump-speech-save-america-rally-transcript-january-6.

3. Quoted in "Donald Trump Speech 'Save America' Rally Transcript January 6."

The insurrection at the U.S. Capitol showed how words can be used to incite violence, even in the most secure places in America.

problem. Then they can organize effectively to counter bad attitudes, possibly change them, and forge solidarity against the forces of intolerance.[5]

However, just because something is legal does not always mean it is the right thing to do. Words matter, and they have consequences. In the case of incitement, for example, words can mean the difference between a peaceful protest and a deadly insurrection.

Rising Up for Rights

Free speech is an essential part of peaceable protests, or events in which people gather together and promote their beliefs. Protesters hope to persuade other people to support their opinions. Often, people protest against decisions the government has made in an effort to get the decision reversed.

Many protests in the United States are peaceful demonstrations, such as this Black Lives Matter candlelight vigil, or nighttime prayer event.

In the United States, people can voice their opinions in a public forum and openly criticize the government because the First Amendment also protects the freedom to assemble and the freedom of speech.

Protests were very common during the 1960s. Some people protested against the unjust treatment of Black people. Others protested for women's rights. Many protested against the United States fighting in the Vietnam War (1954–1975). Although protests are protected under the Constitution, they can sometimes become dangerous. Protests often result in heated feelings on both sides. Because of these feelings, sometimes protests become violent. Although protests are protected by the Constitution, protesters can be arrested if they break other laws. Even peaceful protesters may be at risk for violence when police feel threatened.

During the spring and summer of 2020, there were many protests and demonstrations around the United States calling for an end to unequal, violent policing and racism. More than 7,750 Black Lives Matter demonstrations took place between May and August 2020, and a report by the Armed Conflict Location & Event Data Project (ACLED) found that 93 percent of them were peaceful. However, outrage over the small percentage of violence and looting led to many arrests and public condemnation from some groups and made some people think the heavy police crackdown that summer was justified. This shows how crucial it is for protesters to understand the importance of following laws when they demonstrate.

Arts and Entertainment

Some people are disturbed by violence and questionable images in movies and on television. Some people are highly critical of objectionable language in music. However, freedom of speech also applies to arts and entertainment. Though there have been instances of censorship in American history for questionable content, many people see freedom of expression in music, movies, TV, and other forms of media as an essential American right. The ACLU said:

A free society is based on the principle that each and every individual has the right to decide what art or entertainment he or she wants—or does not want—to receive or create. Once you allow the government to censor someone else, you cede to it the power to censor you, or something you like. Censorship is like poison gas: a powerful weapon that can harm you when the wind shifts.[6]

Even if something is legal, should people be held responsible for its consequences? Groups such as the American Academy of Pediatrics and the American Medical Association have shown concern that violent entertainment, such as books, music, and video games, can lead to violence. In particular, they are concerned that young people may commit violent acts after exposure to violent entertainment. There have been a number of studies on children's exposure to violent video games. There is no conclusive link between violent media and violent behavior, but some studies point to an increase in aggression by children exposed to violence. As a result, many people believe that the government should limit the violent content in certain forms of entertainment, while others believe this is censorship.

Determining Decency

Free expression is sometimes limited if some people find it indecent. The difficulty with this concept is determining what is decent and what is not. Countries that protect free expression try to balance decency and freedom.

The U.S. courts have ruled that the First Amendment protects indecent material. It cannot be banned entirely; however, it may be restricted to protect children. The Federal Communications Commission (FCC), a government organization that regulates television, radio, and the internet, restricts what can be aired on broadcast television and radio stations and at what time. For example, indecent material cannot be aired during the day when young children may be watching.

Some instances of obscenity (that which is considered disgusting, repulsive, or immoral) aren't protected by the First Amendment. The Supreme Court ruled that the First Amendment does not protect obscenity during the *Miller v. California* case in 1973, when Marvin Miller, the owner of a pornographic mail-order company, was convicted for mailing out brochures with pornography on them to advertise his business. The Court also developed "the Miller test" to decide if something is obscene. There are

Violent Media and Young People

Mass school shootings are a huge issue in the United States. In fact, the United States leads the world in mass school shootings. School gun violence hit a peak in 2018, with 94 instances recorded by the U.S. Naval Postgraduate School. Teachers, students, and staff feared for their lives. People often want to figure out why so many young people are turning to gun violence. In search of an explanation for why these events keep happening, some people have pointed to violence in books, movies, television, and video games.

Video games are one of the more controversial forms of entertainment. This is because some simulate graphic violence. Some video games are in a category called "first-person shooter." These games, such as the *Call of Duty* games, allow the player to commit violence from the point of view of a gunman. The game is visually realistic and violently explicit. After the 2012 school shooting at Sandy Hook Elementary, police found that the shooter was an avid player of the *Call of Duty* games.

Should these games be banned? Some people think so. However, that would go against the First Amendment, and some might argue it would amount to censorship. Because of concerns about video games, such as *Call of Duty* and *Grand Theft Auto*, the U.S. video game industry has developed its own ratings system. A game rated "Teen" is for ages 13 and up. "Mature" ratings are for games considered suitable only for ages 17 and older and may include more intense violence, profanity, and mature sexual themes. "Adults Only" games are intended for people older than 18 and may include graphic depictions of sex and violence. It is not illegal for minors, or people under the age of 18, to buy these games, but many retailers refuse

three conditions that must be met. The first is that most average people would consider the work offensive. The second is that the work depicts or describes sexual conduct or bodily functions in an offensive way. The third is that the work, as a whole, lacks serious literary, artistic, political, or scientific value.

While some people debate decency and obscenity when it comes to the First Amendment, one thing is never legal—child pornography. This is any visual depiction of sexually explicit conduct involving a minor (under 18 years old). Creating, importing, selling, buying, or keeping child pornography goes against U.S. federal law and has serious consequences.

to sell adult-rated games to minors who do not have parental permission.

Some states did pass laws that banned the sale of violent video games to minors. The courts, however, have overruled these laws. For example, in 2011, California tried to ban the sale of violent video games to minors, but the Supreme Court ruled that this was unconstitutional. Although the debate about violent entertainment continues, to date, the courts have supported the belief that video games showing violence are protected by the Constitution. Journalist Phil Boffey argued that while video games can be needlessly and horrifically gruesome and violent, young people in other countries play them without acting on the violence they see. He wrote:

Call of Duty is a popular first-person shooter video game with heavy violence.

> *Focusing on violent video games as the cause of mass shootings almost certainly distracts legislators and government officials from the pressing need to deal with more fundamental causes. It is a moral imperative for federal and state legislators, government officials, and all others concerned with lethal violence to confront the underlying problems and not take symbolic refuge in blaming violent video games.*[1]

1. Philip M. Boffey, *Do Violent Video Games Lead to Violence?* Dana Foundation, November 1, 2019, dana.org/article/do-violent-video-games-lead-to-violence/.

Book Banning and Censorship

What does the *Harry Potter* series have in common with *The Grapes of Wrath*? Both were banned in parts of the United States. Book banning is a form of censorship that has been debated for nearly as long as books have existed. It occurs in countries with a lot of government restriction, as well as countries with a lot of freedom. Classics such as Harper Lee's *To Kill a Mockingbird*, Anne Frank's *The Diary of a Young Girl*, and Mark Twain's *The Adventures of Huckleberry Finn* have been banned from libraries and schools because people have disagreed with their content. Author Stephen

The Diary of a Young Girl by Anne Frank is taught in many schools as an important biography from the Holocaust. However, some schools have banned it for sexual themes and even for being too depressing.

Chbosky said, "Banning books gives us silence when we need speech. It closes our ears when we need to listen. It makes us blind when we need sight."[7] Many argue against banning books, saying that if people don't have access to a book, it can be lost to that school and place forever.

The Supreme Court has ruled that banning books in public schools violates the First Amendment. This is because the government funds public schools, and an agency supported by the government cannot interfere with free expression. This was decided during the 1982 *Board of Education, Island Trees School District v. Pico* case.

In 2003, an Arkansas school board voted to remove all of the books in J. K. Rowling's *Harry Potter* series from the district's public school libraries for containing witchcraft, disrespect for authority, and disobedience. Students could only check out these books with written parental permission. Students and parents filed a case because they wanted the books returned to the shelves. The Arkansas judge ordered the books returned to the library shelves, ruling that books could not be banned just because some people disagreed with their content. One outspoken critic of book banning is also a victim of it—author Salman Rushdie. He said, "One of the strange things about free speech is if you live in a free society in which, broadly speaking, you have free speech, you don't think about it that often. Just like if there's enough air, you don't think about the air."[8] Many Muslims were angered by Rushdie's 1988 book *The Satanic Verses*, and it was banned in India. He had to hide for many years because people were calling for his execution.

Free Speech Online

The internet, and especially the rise of social media, has led to many issues around free speech. People can post and view nearly anything on public spaces of the internet. Some people believe that what can be placed online should be limited. They are concerned that children can go on the internet and see indecent and even obscene material.

Because of this concern, the U.S. Congress passed the Communications Decency Act in 1996. This law was meant to protect minors from harmful material on the internet. Specifically, the law made it a crime to post indecent or clearly offensive material anywhere a minor could see it.

Free speech advocates brought the case to court in *Reno v. American Civil Liberties Union*. They were against the part of the act that related to indecent, not obscene, material. They argued that indecent expression is protected under the First Amendment; therefore, it should have no restrictions on the internet. The Supreme Court heard the case in 1997. It ruled that restricting the posting of indecent material on the internet was unconstitutional because it forced the removal of material that adults had a right to see.

Three years later, Congress passed another law to restrict internet access. The courts upheld this law. The Children's Internet Protection Act (CIPA) states that government-funded schools and libraries must filter obscene pictures and pornography shown on the internet. In 2003, the Supreme Court heard a case about CIPA. The Court stated that filters do not violate the Constitution, especially since libraries could turn off the filters upon request.

Another threat to free speech on the internet is the concept of net neutrality—rules put in place to prevent internet service providers (ISPs) from charging more for certain content. In February 2015, the FCC ruled in favor of net neutrality; as *USA Today* explained, "An ISP will be prohibited from slowing the delivery of a TV show simply because it's streamed by a video company that competes with a subsidiary [company owned by] of the ISP."[9] Several ISPs protested the ruling, claiming that net neutrality unconstitutionally limits what they can do as a company. However, individual citizens cheered the ruling because they were worried ISPs would begin limiting content they did not agree with, taking the power of internet surfing out of the hands of individuals.

Protecting Free Press

In some countries, the government controls the news stories that people can read and watch. Many countries crack down on reporters who write or say anything critical of government officials or policies. In fact, more than a third of all people in the world live in countries without a free press. In these countries, it is often dangerous to report unflattering news about the government. According to the International News Safety Institute, more than

Social Media Changes the Conversation

When Facebook launched in 2004, no one could guess how the popular social media platform—as well as Twitter, Instagram, TikTok, and others—would shape our everyday lives. As of 2020, more than 3.6 billion people use social media around the world for connecting with friends and family, managing businesses, and even shaping political discussions and campaigns. It is an amazing tool, which gives everyone a voice. However, there are also questions around free speech when it comes to social media. People can have just a few followers or millions of followers. This gives some people a huge platform for their speech. Free speech is also protected on social media, so people can post anything, as long as it isn't an imminent threat of violence. However, what if someone is using their social media platform to spread hateful ideas or post obscenities? What if someone posts disinformation?

These issues came to the forefront in 2020, as the COVID-19 pandemic spread around the world. Misinformation campaigns on social media harmed health campaigns that tried to get people to stay distant and wear masks. Some people, citing information from their peers on social media, even thought the pandemic was a "hoax." Later in the year, when Joe Biden won the U.S. presidential election, a wide disinformation campaign around election fraud led to many Americans not trusting in the U.S. election results.

After the January 6, 2021, siege at the U.S. Capitol by Trump supporters who believed the election was stolen, Trump lost his privilege to use Twitter, Instagram, Facebook, and other social media sites. Some people argued that this was censorship. However, since Trump had incited violence through his online platforms and since social media companies are private businesses and not owned by the government, suspending him from those services was well within the rights of the social media companies.

50 journalists were killed around the world in 2020 in countries such as Syria, Mexico, and Afghanistan. More were threatened, imprisoned, or tortured. Some of this violence was because reporters were reporting news not approved by the government.

Some people have argued that local journalism might be the way to fight disinformation campaigns.

A free press is a major part of democracy. This civil liberty is covered by the First Amendment. In the United States and most democracies, freedom of the press is guaranteed. This means the government cannot interfere with what newspapers, magazines, or television news programs report.

Although the United States guarantees free press, there are some restrictions. The media cannot maliciously lie about a person in print, which is called libel. When it comes to respecting privacy, courts have generally ruled that journalists have the right to report anything that is arguably of interest to their readers. However, what is of interest is up for debate. In some court cases about privacy, the rulings have favored the press; in others, they have favored the person who feels their privacy has been invaded.

Overall, the United States maintains freedom of the press. Americans believe that freedom of the press, along with the right to assemble and freedom of speech, keeps power in the hands of the people. In recent years, the phrase "fake news" has invaded public conversations around the media. People on both ends of the political spectrum often regard online and print publications that lean away from their own views as false. This has led to some people mistrusting certain publications and questioning the truth behind their news stories. Still, many journalists feel an obligation to print and post the truth, even if they are criticized—and they have every right to in the United States.

Your Opinion Matters!

1. Why is it important that all Americans are able to criticize the government publicly, even if you don't agree with them?

2. What kinds of speech do you think amount to "fighting words" and should be restricted?

3. Do you think disinformation should be protected as free speech even if it causes harm to public health and national security?

CHAPTER THREE

THE RIGHT TO RELIGION

Freedom of religion was one of the major reasons for the arrival of some of the earliest British colonists in the New World. In fact, many people aboard the *Mayflower*, known today as Pilgrims, were from a radical religious sect that sought the freedom to worship God in their own way. These believers, called Separatists, had been persecuted at home in England for illegally breaking with the Church of England. Upon landing in Massachusetts, Separatists and others aboard the *Mayflower* signed the Mayflower Compact, one of the founding documents of American democracy.

Today, freedom of religion is still very important to many Americans. While the United States is a predominantly Christian nation, there is no official national religion. In fact, Christianity is on the decline; in 2019, the Pew Research Center found that only 65 percent of Americans described themselves as Christian, which was down 12 percent in just a decade. The United States is also home to followers of Islam, Judaism, Hinduism, Buddhism, Sikhism, paganism, and more. Some people are atheists, or don't believe in God, and others are agnostic, or believe that nothing is known or can be known about God. The government protects the right of its citizens to freely practice any faith or no faith at all. Freedom of religion also means the

COVID-19 impacted how people practice their religion. In 2020, the Supreme Court ruled against a restriction on religious gatherings in parts of New York with high rates of COVID-19.

government is not allowed to make laws based on any religion. This protects people who do not follow a particular religion from being forced to abide by laws they may not believe in.

Other countries also protect religious freedom. Most of these nations are democracies. While the United States attempts to keep the government and religion completely separate, some countries protect religious freedom but still allow religion to play a role in the government. Separation of church and state is a very important value in the United States so that no one is persecuted or treated unfairly for their religion.

Countries without Freedom of Religion

While religious freedom is an important civil liberty in the United States, it is not protected everywhere in the world. In certain countries, citizens must follow the government-sanctioned religion. In these countries, religion is often tied to how the country is run. In Saudi Arabia, for example, the Quran—the Muslim holy book—is the law of the country. By law, all Saudi citizens must be Muslims and follow the laws of the Quran. The government punishes those who practice other religions.

China is another country with little religious freedom. The ruling party of China, the Chinese Communist Party, is officially atheist, and it prohibits its members from holding religious beliefs. Officially, China guarantees freedom of religion under its constitution, but religions must be approved and religious gatherings must be supervised by government officials. Some groups meet secretly, but they may be arrested if they are discovered. In recent years, the Chinese government has faced more accusations that it is limiting Christians' religious freedom. In 2018, the *New York Times* reported about China's anti-religious policies:

> [Xi Jinping], *apparently concerned that independent worship might pose a threat to the ruling Communist Party's dominance over daily life in China, has sought to bring Christianity more firmly under the party's control. The government this year banned online sales of the Bible, burned crosses, demolished churches and forced at least a half-dozen places of worship to close.*[1]

China has also been accused of leading a genocide against Uighur Muslims, knocking down mosques, banning Muslim religious dress, and detaining people for "re-education." China counters that it safeguards religious freedom, but religious organizations must follow the laws of the country, which include registering the organization through the government and following the government's procedures. The government claims their laws protect both religious freedom and national order.

Protected by the Constitution

The First Amendment prevents the U.S. government from interfering in a person's religious choices. The first clause of the amendment is the Establishment Clause, which states that "Congress shall make no law respecting an establishment of religion."[2] This means that the government cannot set up a state religion. It also cannot give privileges to one religion over another. This is often referred to as the separation of church and state, or secularism. Thomas Jefferson, in an 1802 letter to the Danbury Baptist Association, wrote, "I contemplate with sovereign reverence that act of the whole American people which declared that their legislature should 'make no law respecting an establishment of religion, or prohibiting the free exercise thereof,' thus building a wall of separation between Church and State."[3] The Supreme Court has ruled in many cases to uphold the Establishment Clause, including in *County of Allegheny v. ACLU* (1989), which ruled that a nativity scene outside a government building violated the clause. *Burstyn v. Wilson* in 1952 ruled that the government couldn't censor a motion picture because it is considered offensive to religious beliefs.

The First Amendment continues with the Free Exercise Clause. This clause keeps Congress from standing in the way of a free exercise of religion. This part of the amendment means that the government cannot interfere with a person's religious practices as long as the practices are legal.

One difficulty with these clauses is that they can clash. On one side, the government must try to ensure that people can freely practice their religions. On the other side, the government has to be

Limits to Religious Expression

Some countries try to limit religious expression in public. France, Austria, Belgium, and other countries have banned some forms of religious dress, especially full-body coverings (burkas or burqas) and face-covering garments (niqabs). In 2016, some French beach towns restricted the right of women to wear a burkini, a type of modest swimwear that covers the body and hair. The ban was said to protect secularism. Many women in burkinis were fined and told to leave the beaches. One woman was made to take off her covering in front of the police. Knowledge of the ban spread through the Western world, leading to demonstrations from Muslims and women in France and around the world. People declared the ban to be an infringement of the rights of people to dress how they like as well as an infringement of religious freedom. The highest court in France agreed and quickly overturned the ban, stating that it violated civil liberties. Some Western nations have kept Muslim women wearing traditional coverings from working in government jobs or receiving public services. Some people believe banning this type of religious dress will help immigrants to assimilate and will keep people safe from attackers. However, others argue that such rules discriminate against Muslim women, many of whom see their face and body coverings as a religious obligation. When the Canadian province of Quebec banned face coverings in 2017, Ihsaan Gardee, the executive director of the National Council of Canadian Muslims, said it was "an unnecessary law with a made-up solution to an invented problem."[1]

This is an example of a burkini, which was banned in France in 2016 following Islamic extremist terrorist attacks.

1. Quoted in Liam Stack, "Burqa Bans: Which Countries Outlaw Face Coverings?" *New York Times*, October 19, 2017, www. nytimes.com/2017/10/19/world/europe/quebec-burqa-ban-europe.html.

sure that it does not promote a certain religion when protecting this right. Keeping this balance is not always easy.

Religion in Public Schools

Public schools receive their funding from the government, so they must follow constitutional laws around religion. The debate over whether to teach creationism, evolution, or both has been an ongoing debate in schools. Creationism is the belief that God created the world exactly as stated in the Bible. Creationists get this belief from some Christian religious teachings and believe creationism should be taught in schools. Evolution is a scientific theory that all life today is the result of many changes that have happened over millions of years. This is based on scientific evidence and research.

Some parents believe that evolution conflicts with their religious beliefs. They think that their children should not be taught about evolution. Other parents believe that creationism should not be taught in public schools. They think this is the government mandating religion.

For years, teachers taught creationism in schools. However, when scientists such as Charles Darwin made great strides in understanding the development of humans and the natural world, evolutionary science advanced. By the 1900s, more people wanted evolution taught in public schools. However, many religious people were offended by the theory of evolution. By 1925, some states had passed laws that made it illegal to teach evolution in schools. As the years passed, the laws against evolution were contested, and eventually the courts overturned them. They allowed for evolution to be taught to students because it is a scientific theory.

In 1987, the U.S. Supreme Court ruled in *Edwards v. Aguillard* that it was unconstitutional to require creationism to be taught in public schools. Because creationism is a religious view, it violates the Establishment Clause. However, creationism can be discussed in classes about religious theory. The Anti-Defamation League wrote, "Religious explanations for humankind, the diversity of life on earth, or the universe, including Creationism, Creation Science, or Intelligent Design may not be taught as science under any circumstances.

Prayer in School

Do you think students should be forced to pray in public school? While the right to practice religion is part of the First Amendment, it sometimes clashes with the Establishment Clause, or separation of church and state.

Some public schools have devoted a few minutes each day to silent prayer. While some people believe that school prayer is a right guaranteed by the Free Exercise Clause, others believe school prayer is a violation of the Establishment Clause. They think that if a public school devotes time to prayer, it is an example of the government imposing religion on students.

The American courts have ruled on the matter. In 1962, the U.S. Supreme Court banned school-sponsored prayer in public schools. Mandated school prayer in public schools violates the First Amendment. However, courts have allowed a moment of silence in public schools, and students are allowed to pray silently to themselves; religion is permitted as long as no one is forced into doing something they do not want to do. In 2000, Virginia enacted a law that required a moment of silence. Students may choose to pray, meditate, or just sit quietly during this time. Some parents and students challenged this

Evolution—the only scientific explanation for the history of life on earth—must only be taught as scientific fact."[4]

Another religious issue in public schools is how to preserve students' personal freedom to express their beliefs while not inflicting their views on their classmates. Basically, students can express their beliefs in their homework, artwork, and other assignments. They can talk about religious beliefs with their classmates. Students can pray at school as long as it does not interfere with school functions. They can wear clothing that expresses their religious viewpoints. Students can also set up religious clubs.

In the United States, public school teachers are allowed to pray and read the Bible or other religious works as long as they do so privately and on their own time. Additionally, they cannot impose their beliefs on others. They may discuss religion in class, but it must be pertinent to the subject, such as a religion's impact on art, history, or culture, and they cannot equate any religious ideas with the "truth."

law, claiming it was unconstitutional because even a moment of silence implies prayer and promotes religion. The case went to a federal appeals court. The court found that the law did not violate the First Amendment because the law did not require prayer or promote it.

In 2020, President Trump sought to defend prayer in public schools and threatened to cut federal funds to schools that violate their students' rights to religious expression. His order didn't change the precedents already set forth by law, but it drew attention to the concerns of religious people—especially his Evangelical Christian supporters—who wanted the security to freely express their faith.

Praying is important to some young people, and not to others. No one can be forced to pray in public schools in the United States.

Religion in Private School

Private schools don't have to follow all of the rules pertaining to the Establishment Clause because they are funded by others (often the parents of the children who attend them) and not the government. Things that are not allowed in public schools, such as mandatory prayer, restrictions on free speech, and discrimination based on sexual orientation can be allowed in a private school.

However, this does not mean private schools allow everything public schools do not. Private school students still enjoy many basic civil liberties. For example, it is illegal for staff to hurt students, and schools are not allowed to deny students entry based on race. Additionally, each state has its own rules regarding private schools. For example, most states do not regulate private schools' testing policies.

Another heated issue regarding religion and education involves school vouchers. A school voucher is a certificate issued by the government that parents can use to send their children to a school of

Reciting the Pledge

Have you ever recited the U.S. Pledge of Allegiance? It refers to the United States as "one nation, under God."[1] Many public schools devote time in the morning to reciting the pledge. However, is this constitutional, since referring to a Christian God in public school may violate separation of church and state?

Some parents believe that reciting the pledge violates the Establishment Clause. They feel that a public school should not make students recite a pledge with God in it. By doing so, they reason, the government is imposing religion on people. Others believe that the pledge is not religious and reciting "under God" is just a tradition.

In 1943, the Supreme Court heard *West Virginia Board of Education v. Barnette*. Since the words "under God" had not yet been added to the pledge at this point, the case was not about religious freedom; it was about whether students should be required to recite the pledge at all. The Court ruled that students should be able to opt out of the pledge. Although students have this right, some people still feel that saying it at school violates the Establishment Clause. Cases regarding the pledge continue to go to court. In 2014, a New Jersey family and the American Humanist Society filed to have "under God" removed from the pledge, stating that it "marginalizes atheist and humanist kids as something less than ideal patriots."[2] They lost the case in 2015, when a state judge ruled in favor of the school district and Samantha Jones, a teen who argued that removing the words from the pledge would take away her right to say the pledge in full.

1. "The Pledge of Allegiance," Washington Secretary of State, www.sos.wa.gov/flag/pledge.aspx (accessed March 11, 2021).

2. American Humanist Association, Press Release, April 21, 2014, americanhumanist.org/press-releases/2014-04-humanists-file-lawsuit-against-under-god-in-the-pled/.

their choice, including private schools, using government funding. One reason why school vouchers are controversial is because parents have used them to send their children to religious schools. Some people believe that once the government gives parents the voucher, it's up to the parents to determine whether they want their children to receive a religious education. Others believe that government funding should not be used to support religious schools in any way. Frank S. Ravitch, Professor of Law at Michigan State University, said, "Rather than preventing religious discrimination … [school vouchers] may actually support a system that discriminates against religious minorities and those of no faith."[5]

When Betsy DeVos became the U.S. secretary of education in 2017, one of her goals was to create a national school voucher program, so parents could choose to send their child to a private school with tax-funded money. Some people agreed with this policy because it would allow parents to decide which school was best for their child, regardless of their socioeconomic background or address. Others railed against the policy, saying it would take tax dollars away from struggling public schools and would take away from the right to secular education for all children.

Are Religious Displays Okay?

The Supreme Court first heard a case about public religious displays in 1980. The case was about a Kentucky law that required public schools to display the Ten Commandments. The court determined that the law was government sponsorship of religion, and it was ruled unconstitutional. In another religious display case four years later, there was a different outcome. In *Lynch v. Donnelly*, the Court ruled that a Christmas nativity scene displayed in the municipal square of Pawtucket, Rhode Island, was acceptable because it also displayed secular symbols of Christmas, like reindeer. This set a precedent called the "reindeer rule." The Court reasoned that the scene recognized the history of Christmas, and it noted that Christmas has both secular and religious significance. The justices concluded that the display did not mean that the government endorsed Christianity.

The Pew Forum on Religion and Public Life found in a 2005 survey that 83 percent of Americans approved of Christmas symbols on government property, saying, "Each year as the winter holidays approach, Americans across the country debate the appropriateness of the government sponsoring, or even permitting, the display

Some might say this nativity scene on Capitol Hill violates the Establishment Clause. What do you think?

of Christmas nativity scenes, Hanukkah menorahs and other religious holiday symbols on public property."[6] Some people believe that these displays are harmless celebrations of the holiday season. Other people argue that the displays mean that the government is sponsoring religion. While it's fine for a business to decorate for a holiday, a city hall's nativity decorations may seem to toe the line of the Establishment Clause.

The conflict between the Court's rulings reflects the conflict Americans feel about church-and-state issues. According to a 2014 Pew Research Center survey, 44 percent of American adults believe Christian symbols should be allowed on government property. Another 28 percent say Christian symbols should be allowed only if they are accompanied by symbols from other faiths. In this case, a Christian nativity scene is fine, as long as a Jewish menorah accompanies it. Only 20 percent of Americans believe religious symbols should be completely banned from government property.

The First Amendment provides the guidance for how issues should be treated, but it can be interpreted in different ways. The U.S. government strives to follow the amendment's guidance, balancing both clauses.

When Religion Violates Rights

In 1993, Congress passed the Religious Freedom Restoration Act, which prohibits any agency, department, or official of a U.S. federal or state government to burden a person's exercise of religion. However, sometimes protecting one person's civil liberties leads to violating another person's civil liberties. For example, a baker may refuse to make a wedding cake for a same-sex couple because they believe gay marriage is against their religion. A Catholic hospital may limit essential reproductive health services, such as contraception, because it goes against church teachings.

In 2014, the Supreme Court ruled in *Burwell v. Hobby Lobby* that requiring family-owned corporations to pay for insurance coverage for contraception under the Patient Protection and Affordable Care Act violated religious freedoms. Justice Ruth Bader Ginsburg voted against this ruling, writing, "The court's expansive notion of corporate personhood invites for-profit entities to seek religion-based exemptions from regulations they deem offensive to their faiths."[7] She said that this could set a dangerous precedent in which corporations could object to health coverage of vaccines, equal pay for women, and even the minimum wage.

In 2015, a Kentucky clerk named Kim Davis refused to issue marriage licenses for same-sex couples because of her religion. She was briefly jailed and sued because her religious ideas had violated other peoples' rights. James Esseks, director of the ACLU's LGBT & HIV Project said, "When you do a job on behalf of the government—as an employee or a contractor—there is no license to discriminate or turn people away because they do not meet religious criteria. Our government could not function if everyone doing the government's business got to pick their own rules."[8] Debates about religious liberty and other civil liberties will likely be part of the U.S. government for many years to come.

Your Opinion Matters!

1. Why do you think it's important to uphold freedom of religion in a multicultural society?

2. In what cases, if any, do you think religious displays or clothing should be restricted?

3. Do you think private companies should be able to discriminate against other people based on something that goes against the companies' religion?

ENSURING SAFETY AND SECURITY

What is more important: upholding a person's individual civil liberties or keeping other people safe? This is a question that all levels of government have to deal with. Some people support measures they believe will help the government keep citizens safe, even when those measures violate civil liberties. This is especially true in the case of terrorism; many Americans fear terrorists—both foreign and domestic—and believe the government should be able to investigate anyone for any reason if it helps catch terrorists before they can hurt people. These people generally feel that government surveillance is not a problem because innocent people have nothing to hide and therefore, nothing to fear from the government. Some people believe that there should be tight restrictions on owning deadly weapons, such as guns, which can be used to kill a great number of innocent people if they fall into the wrong hands.

However, many others believe that there is no excuse for violating people's rights in the name of national security. Some fear the government constantly spying on their private information. In the case of owning guns, some people believe the Second Amendment ensures the right of any American to own any gun they want, and they don't want the government interfering in their ability to purchase it.

A look through American history shows moments where it was deemed necessary to limit civil liberties for what the government

People protested against gun violence at the March for Our Lives on March 24, 2018.

claimed was a good cause. While civil liberties are important, so is national security and the safety of the American people.

A History of Limited Liberties

Throughout history, the U.S. government has limited civil liberties in order to maintain national security, generally during times of war or threat of war. Often, the restrictions were repealed when the threat was over.

In 1798, when the new United States was on the verge of war with France, the Alien and Sedition Acts were signed into law. Sedition is speech or behavior meant to incite people to rebel against the authority of a state. The acts allowed officials to jail people if they published anything malicious about the U.S. government. When the threat of war was over, the acts were repealed. Supporters of the acts claimed they were needed to suppress French sympathizers and their attempts to weaken the U.S. government.

In 1918, after the United States joined World War I, the government passed the Sedition Act, which imposed serious penalties on anyone found guilty of insulting or abusing the government, flag, Constitution, or military; getting in the way of the production of war materials; or making false statements about the war, among other things. It was aimed at socialists and pacifists (people who oppose war).

After World War I, Communists took control of Russia, and some Americans supported the Communist Party in the United States. Some Americans became afraid of Communism and believed that Communists wanted to overthrow the American government. This was known as the Red Scare. "The nation was gripped in fear," wrote attorney Paul Burnett. "Innocent people were jailed for expressing their views, civil liberties were ignored, and many Americans feared that a Bolshevik-style [Russian-style] revolution was at hand."[1]

World War II brought more violations of civil liberties. In 1941, Japan attacked the United States. The U.S. government was afraid that anyone of Japanese heritage living in the United States would spy on the government. The U.S. military forced approximately 120,000 Japanese Americans out of their homes and sent them to prison camps. President Franklin Roosevelt—the same president who promised to guard the

Civil War and Security

In 1861, as the American Civil War was beginning, President Abraham Lincoln suspended habeas corpus. This legal act protects people from being unlawfully detained or held in prison without charges being filed and without giving the accused some recourse to address the charges. The writ of habeas corpus has historically been used to protect an individual's freedom against government detention.

President Lincoln's suspension of habeas corpus allowed the military to detain people it thought threatened the country's security even if they could not be charged with a crime. The courts reinstated habeas corpus after the American Civil War, but at the time, it was deemed necessary to suspend it for the good of the country. Lincoln declared:

Now, therefore, be it ordered, that during the existing insurrection, and as a necessary measure for suppressing the same, all rebels and insurgents, their aiders and abettors within the United States, and all persons discouraging volunteer enlistments, resisting militia drafts, or guilty of any disloyal practice affording aid and comfort to the rebels against the authority of the United States, shall be subject to martial law, and liable to trial and punishment by courts-martial or military commission.[1]

1. Abraham Lincoln, "Domestic Intelligence: A Proclamation," *Harper's Weekly*, October 11, 1862, www.sonofthesouth.net/leefoundation/civil-war/1862/october/lincoln-writ-habeas-corpus.htm.

This illustration shows Abraham Lincoln reading the Emancipation Proclamation to his Cabinet members. Lincoln led the United States through one of its darkest times—the Civil War.

Japanese Americans were forced to relocate to internment camps, such as Manzanar (*pictured here*), during World War II.

liberties of all citizens— signed the executive order that allowed this to happen. "The imprisonment of almost all of the country's citizens of Japanese ancestry, which occurred without a single documented case of treasonable conduct by a Japanese-American, is one of the worst civil liberties abuses in American history,"[2] wrote Christopher Finan, former president of the American Booksellers Foundation for Free Expression. Toward the end of the war, the Supreme Court ruled that detaining loyal citizens violated the Constitution. In 1945, the camps were closed. The Civil Liberties Act of 1987 acknowledged the "grave injustice" done to citizens of Japanese ancestry "without security reasons and without any acts of espionage or sabotage" and "motivated by racial prejudice, wartime hysteria and a failure of political leadership."[3]

Just a few years after World War II, the government violated civil liberties during another Red Scare. The Cold War, which began during this time, was a standoff between the United States and the Soviet Union, which included what is now Russia. Because Russia was a Communist country, members of the Communist Party in the United States were victimized for their beliefs. U.S. Senator Joseph McCarthy conducted hearings and persecuted people suspected of being Communists. People lost their jobs and were even imprisoned because of their political beliefs. The harassment became known as McCarthyism. People accused of being Communists took their cases to court. In most cases, the courts found the government's actions unconstitutional. McCarthy was later criticized for his actions.

Gun Control and Civil Liberties

One of the most controversial issues in the United States for the past century has been gun control. The Second Amendment to the U.S. Constitution states, "The right of the people to keep and bear Arms, shall not be infringed."[4] However, that law was made in a different time, with different concerns, and different technology. Some people think that doesn't matter, and the right to bear arms is still a civil liberty that should not be limited. Other people think that national security and public safety need to be taken into account, especially now that fire-arms are much more powerful than they were more than 200 years ago when the Constitution was written.

There was nearly no gun control legislation until 1934 when the government attempted to crack down on violent gangs with the National Firearms Act. It required federal registration of certain types of fire-arms. Gun dealers, manufacturers, and importers were now required to have firearms licenses, and sales of guns to some people, including people convicted of a felony, were banned. In 1968, Congress passed the Gun Control Act, which created new categories of firearms crimes and banned the sale of firearms to felons and other groups of people. This was in response to high-profile assassinations of President John F. Kennedy and his brother, Senator Robert Kennedy, as well as Martin Luther King Jr. In 1993, legislation was passed requiring federal back-ground checks before firearms could be bought from federally licensed dealers. The following year, large capacity ammunition magazines and semi-automatic assault weapons were banned, though the act expired only 10 years later and wasn't renewed. In the past 20 years, gun rights have increased and federal restrictions are often not passed, aided by campaigns by the National Rifle Association (NRA). Some jurisdictions allow people to openly carry their guns, while others prohibit it.

Some people argue that more gun control is needed. In 2011, Con-gresswoman Gabby Giffords was shot in the head by a gunman, who also shot 18 other people at a political event. She founded the Giffords Law Center to Prevent Gun Violence. Giffords Law Center reports that the United States leads high-income nations in gun violence, and at least 200 Americans are shot and injured every day. Mass shootings have become a major issue in recent history.

School shootings are also on the rise, as young people get their hands on guns and use them to violent ends. In 2012, a shooter killed 20 students and 6 adults at Sandy Hook Elementary School in Newtown, Connecticut. In 2018, a gunman killed 17 people at Marjory Stoneman Douglas High School in Parkland, Florida. Students from

Gabby Giffords is now an outspoken advocate for common-sense gun legislation.

this school organized the March for Our Lives for gun control legislation in Washington, D.C., later that year. Survivor Emma González said in a speech, "In a little over six minutes, 17 of our friends were taken from us, 15 were injured, and everyone—absolutely everyone in the Douglas community—was forever altered … Everyone who has been touched by the cold grip of gun violence understands."[5] Despite the march and national outrage over mass shootings, gun violence legislation did not take hold during the Trump administration. In 2019, there were 417 mass shootings in the United States; this included a hate crime in which a shooter targeted Latinx people at a Walmart in El Paso, Texas.

Is there a common ground between people who want gun rights and gun control? Some people believe common sense gun laws will make a difference. Even though she was a victim of gun violence and advocates for gun control, Gabby Giffords believes that gun rights are essential to American civil liberties and identity. She wrote an article in 2013 in which she said:

> As gun owners, my husband and I understand that the Second Amendment is most at risk when a criminal or deranged person commits a gun crime. These acts only embolden those who oppose gun ownership. Promoting responsible gun laws protects the Second Amendment and reduces lives lost from guns.[6]

Heightened Security After 9/11

Certain events in American history have prompted a restriction on citizens' rights to privacy in the name of national security. On September 11, 2001, members of al-Qaeda, an Islamist terrorist group, flew two passenger airliners into the World Trade Center in New York

City. They also brought down a plane in Pennsylvania and crashed another into the Pentagon near Washington, D.C. The terrorists killed nearly 3,000 people and injured 6,000 others.

Following the attacks (often known as the 9/11 attacks), the U.S. government wanted broader powers to avoid future attacks. Government leaders said they needed to be able to more easily investigate a suspected terrorist. They wanted laws that allowed them to use today's technology, such as cell phones and the internet, to investigate suspected terrorists. Government agencies that gathered information about people needed to be able to easily share this information, and they also wanted greater access to people's personal records.

President George W. Bush and other politicians developed the Uniting and Strengthening America by Providing Appropriate Tools Required to Intercept and Obstruct Terrorism Act of 2001. Because the name of the act is an acronym for USA PATRIOT, most people simply call it the Patriot Act. It gives the government more power over national security issues. Many groups, such as the ACLU, argued that the expanded powers would allow the government to invade people's privacy, violate the right to free expression, and restrict due process. Despite these objections, Congress passed the Patriot Act 45 days after the September 11 attacks. Elected officials said that the act was necessary to keep U.S. citizens safe and to catch terrorists before they could attack the country again.

The Patriot Act expanded the government's power to monitor people's activities and records in order to investigate potential terrorists or terrorist activities. For example, the Patriot Act allows federal investigators to authorize "roving" wiretaps. Once authorities get a warrant for a roving wiretap, they can use

The 9/11 terrorist attacks on American soil created trauma and fear for many Americans.

This costume mocks the Patriot Act with the phrase "One Nation Under Surveillance."

it to monitor a suspect's home telephone, cell phone, or computer. Previously, officials needed separate authorization for each device. The Patriot Act also makes it easier for the government to obtain a person's medical, library, financial, student, or mental health records. The Patriot Act allows the government to access a person's personal records held by a third party with relative ease. With the Patriot Act, investigators can look at these records just by saying it is necessary for national security, and they do not have to inform the target of the search.

The Patriot Act also strengthened the ways investigators can deal with terrorist activity involving money. Money laundering is how criminals or terrorists move money without detection and then use the money to help them commit their crimes. The Patriot Act improved the government's ability to detect money laundering by requiring banks to monitor the flow of large sums of money and report any suspicious activity to the Department of the Treasury.

The Debate Over Surveillance

Government surveillance is another controversial issue in the United States, even today, and the effects of the Patriot Act are often debated. What's more important: security or privacy? Some believe the Patriot Act was necessary to update laws so that government agencies could fight terrorism with today's technology. It also allowed for better communication between governmental agencies and tightened airport security. However, there are many parts of the act that people don't agree with.

One of the most controversial aspects of the Patriot Act is that it allows so-called "sneak-and-peek" surveillance. If it gets a search warrant, the Federal Bureau of Investigation (FBI) can search a person's house or business without giving them immediate notice. Later, after the search, the FBI will give the person the warrant. The Justice

Department says that providing notice may jeopardize an investigation. With notice, those investigated may be able to conceal evidence of terrorist activity. Critics say that investigators already had the power to do secret searches in counterterror and counterespionage probes. The problem with this part of the Patriot Act, critics contend, is that it authorizes the use of secret searches for any crime, no matter how minor. This violates people's right to privacy. In 2005, the government confirmed that only 12 percent of sneak-and-peek warrants were related to terrorism; most were actually for drug-related issues.

The Patriot Act also lets the government review people's personal records, even if they are not suspected of a crime. These include health, financial, purchasing, and other records. In the past, a government investigator had to get a warrant to get this information. To get the warrant, the investigator had to go to a federal judge and prove that there was probable cause that a crime had been committed. Now, the official can just go to the Foreign Intelligence Surveillance Court and say that the search involves protecting the country against terrorism. The official does not need to make a case for probable cause. The court gives the investigator a subpoena, which requires the record holder, such as a cell phone company or a bank, to hand over the records. Additionally, the subject of the search does not have to be notified that their records are being reviewed.

A 2005 CBS poll found that 45 percent of Americans felt the Patriot Act went too far and threatened civil liberties. Some revisions were made in 2006 when the law was renewed. In 2007, district judge Ann Aiken ruled that parts of the Patriot Act violate the Constitution because each of those parts "permits the executive branch of government to conduct surveillance and searches of American citizens without satisfying the probable cause requirements of the Fourth Amendment."[7] However, in 2011, 42 percent of Americans still said the Patriot Act was a necessary tool.

Over time, however, these views changed. According to the Pew Research Center, by 2014, 74 percent of Americans said they did not believe it was necessary to give up privacy and freedom for the sake of safety. This was, in part, prompted by the release of classified information by government employee and whistleblower Edward Snowden about National Security Agency (NSA) surveillance programs.

In 2015, the Patriot Act was set to expire. While some parts of the law did expire, others were reissued under a new law called the USA Freedom Act. This act was enacted by Congress on June 2, 2015, and upholds many of the same provisions as the Patriot Act, but with some modifications. The leak of information by Edward Snowden caused Congress to alter the way the NSA could collect information. Phone records are now held by telephone companies instead of bulk collection by the NSA. The government must ask telephone companies for these records, and the companies have the option to deny a request in court. The USA Freedom Act did restore the ability of the government to use roving wiretapping, a practice many people object to. Even if a person changes phone numbers, the government can still collect their phone information and listen in.

Rights of Wartime Prisoners

The Geneva Conventions are international agreements on how to treat prisoners of war, or POWs. Countries that sign the Geneva Conventions agree to treat prisoners humanely and according to rules laid out in the document. One requirement is that countries respect prisoners' religions. The agreements do not permit any degrading treatment.

Up until 2001, the United States followed these conventions with all POWs since they signed the agreement in 1949. However, after the 9/11 attacks, the Bush administration decided that the Geneva Convention did not protect all Afghan and Iraqi prisoners of war.

As the United States went to war in Afghanistan, the Bush administration stated that the Geneva Conventions didn't apply to Afghan POWs because these prisoners were not soldiers from Afghanistan's military. Instead, they were part of a rogue militia, the Taliban, and a terrorist group, al-Qaeda. These prisoners were termed unlawful combatants. As unlawful combatants, these POWs had few rights, so the United States justified torturing them to obtain information.

During the Iraq War, which began in 2003, some U.S. soldiers stationed at Abu Ghraib prison tortured POWs. Pictures, interviews, and films document the physical and mental abuse toward the prisoners.

Snowden Uncovers Surveillance

Under the Patriot Act, the NSA could monitor U.S. citizens without their knowledge. In 2013, a computer programmer inside the NSA named Edward Snowden stole top-secret information about the data being collected. After traveling to Hong Kong for safety, Snowden exposed a program called Prism that allowed the NSA to request telephone records of millions of Americans. No one knew their information was being collected until Snowden leaked the information to the media.

The information also showed that the U.S. government was spying on other nations and gathering data. The leak showed information collected on the heads of different countries, including allies of the United States. Foreign governments demanded an end to the data collection. Snowden was charged with stealing information. Some people have called Snowden a spy and traitor, while others call him a hero. He defended his actions, saying, "I'm willing to sacrifice [my former life] because I can't in good conscience allow the U.S. government to destroy privacy, internet freedom and basic liberties for people around the world with this massive surveillance machine they're secretly building."[1] He is currently living in Russia.

1. Quoted in Glenn Greenwald, Ewen MacAskill, and Laura Poitras, "Edward Snowden: The whistleblower behind the NSA surveillance revelations," *The Guardian*, June 11, 2013, www.theguardian.com/world/2013/jun/09/edward-snowden-nsa-whistleblower-surveillance.

Edward Snowden was seen as a traitor by some and a hero by others.

According to a Red Cross report, military intelligence officers estimate that somewhere between 70 and 90 percent of those whom they detained were picked up by mistake and were not guilty of any crime.

This photograph from Abu Ghraib shows a U.S. soldier using a trained dog to intimidate an Iraqi prisoner.

Some critics claim U.S. government policies made Abu Ghraib possible. Many military personnel who were stationed at Abu Ghraib said the prisoner abuses were part of a general pattern of brutal, uncivil interrogation policy. They said the United States put this policy into place after 9/11. The White House claimed that what happened at Abu Ghraib was an unacceptable occurrence, but investigations showed that some torture orders came from high-ranking government officials.

Some people believed that the government's actions were necessary to deal with potential terrorists. They felt the U.S. government needed more freedom when questioning prisoners who may have been involved in terrorism. Others argued that this abused civil liberties. They contended that all people, no matter what they have done, have natural rights. These include the right not to be tortured and the right to be represented in a court. Additionally, they feared that many innocent men and foot soldiers might be captured and treated the same as hardened terrorists.

Without the Geneva Conventions, the prisoners had no clear rights. This issue caused disagreement even within the Bush administration. Former Secretary of State Colin Powell was among the critics. In a memo, he wrote that the decision to ignore the Geneva Conventions would "reverse over a century of U.S. policy and practice and undermine the protections of the law of war for our troops."[8] Some believe that President Bush's decision led to civil rights abuses. These critics claim that by denying some prisoners rights, the government set a tone that the rights of all POWs could be ignored.

Some prisoners deemed most "dangerous" were held at the detention center at the U.S. Guantánamo Bay Naval Base in Cuba. Critics believed detainees were kept away from the U.S. mainland to limit their ability to be heard in court. The Bush administration said terror suspects did not have the right to come into U.S. courts and demand the rights that U.S. citizens have under the legal system. Instead, the U.S. government

In the United States, even prisoners are supposed to have basic rights.

said that the suspects would receive justice through military tribunals. The government declared them "enemy combatants" in order to deny them the civil liberties POWs have. Some POWs who had been released told of torture within the prison and force feeding when inmates went on hunger strikes. International organizations such as Amnesty International have called for the center to be permanently closed.

From 2001 to 2008, 775 detainees were brought to Guantánamo Bay. By 2016, all but 61 were released without charge. Only one prisoner was actually convicted of a crime. President Barack Obama declared that he would close the prison at Guantánamo Bay during his presidency, but he was unable to accomplish this during his two terms in office. In 2018, President Trump signed an executive order to keep Guantánamo Bay detention center open indefinitely, saying that the United States had to have "all necessary power to detain terrorists."[9]

There's often not an easy way to balance civil liberties and national security. In times of war or after a major terrorist attack, some laws may seem like an example of government overreach, or in the cases of POW treatment in Abu Ghraib and Guantánamo Bay, they can be seen as major human rights issues. It often takes discussion at all levels of government and calls to action from citizens and media to change such laws that restrict civil liberties in the name of security and safety.

Your Opinion Matters!

1. Do you think civil liberties are more important than national security in some cases? When might this be the case?

2. Why might times of war and threats to national security lead to restrictions of civil liberties?

3. Do you think government surveillance goes against a person's right to privacy?

PERSONAL CHOICE AND PRIVACY

In 2020, the entire world was turned upside down as the COVID-19 pandemic started spreading rapidly and claiming lives. Some people called on the United States government to make federal mandates, or rules, for wearing masks, attending gatherings, contact tracing, and even imposing lockdowns. Countries such as China responded with strong restrictions and even used government surveillance methods to put people into categories based on their level of risk of having the virus. Some people argued that the U.S. government enacting such mandates could save thousands, or even hundreds of thousands, of lives.

However, other people railed against government restrictions. They thought it was a personal choice to wear a mask or not, even if wearing one could help the common good. They wanted to travel without restrictions, and they didn't want the government to check up on where they'd gone or who they'd come in contact with. Many were angered by forced quarantines, which aimed to keep the disease from spreading.

The COVID-19 pandemic brought up an important issue with civil liberties. Should personal choices and private matters be regulated or overseen by the government, or should someone be able to do whatever they want, even if it might hurt others directly or indirectly? Debates of personal choice and privacy are much like

◀ Dr. Anthony Fauci, director of the National Institute of Allergy and Infectious Diseases (NIAID), became a leading voice for public health during the COVID-19 pandemic, urging people to wear masks to save lives.

the debates over how national security affects civil liberties. The answer is rarely clear, and the arguments are increasingly polarized.

Right to Privacy

The right to privacy means people have the right to make personal decisions without government interference. Parents are able to choose what TV shows their children can watch, people can decide where to travel, and no one is forced to eat certain foods. They can decide whether they want to get a vaccination or to vaccinate their kids. The right to privacy also protects people's personal documents, records, and property from the government.

Most European countries protect privacy and personal choice. The European Convention on Human Rights guarantees that a person's family life, home, and correspondence should be free from interference. The European Union requires all of its member states to have laws that protect their citizens' right to privacy. The United States also protects the right to privacy in many cases. This right is not explicitly stated in the Bill of Rights. However, diseases such as measles, mumps, and rubella. When he was able to decide for himself, he had to catch up on vaccinations he felt he should have had his whole life. His mother had decided not to vaccinate him based on misinformation, which he felt was dangerous. Lindenberger said, "Using the love, affection, and care of a parent for their children to push an agenda and create false distress is shameful. The sources which spread misinformation should be the primary concern of the American people."[1] Lindenberger's testimony brought national attention to the dangers of anti-vaccine campaigns. In this case, people argue, public health might be more important than personal choice.

Ethan Lindenberger spoke to Congress on March 15, 2019, about the dangers of misinformation in the vaccine debate.

1. Quoted in Gracie Bonds-Staples, "There is no Excuse. Anti-Vaxxers Put Us All at Risk," *The Atlanta Journal-Constitution*, March 12, 2019, www.ajc.com/lifestyles/health/there-excuse-anti-vaxxers-put-all-risk/t63xjfUQWf41x8pNBuFkiK/.

the U.S. Supreme Court has interpreted privacy rights in the First, Fourth, and Fifth Amendments. The Supreme Court has ruled that most personal decisions are private and the government cannot interfere with these.

Some countries, such as Zimbabwe, do not protect the right to privacy. Although Zimbabwe's constitution states that it protects privacy, its laws conflict with this statement. In August 2007, the president of Zimbabwe signed into law the Interception of Communications Act. This act gives the government the authority to eavesdrop on people's phone calls and read their mail and email. The country's communication minister can approve the surveillance of people's correspondence without getting court approval. Basically, the government has the authority to eavesdrop on anyone for any reason.

LGBTQ+ Rights and Privacy

In recent years, rights for LGBTQ+ individuals have grown in the United States. Same-sex marriage is legal, a person can't be discriminated against for their sexuality in the workplace, and openly LGBTQ+ people are able to serve in the military. However, for much of U.S. history, and still in some places around the world, homosexuality was illegal even though it dealt with the most private of matters—a person's relationships.

Until only a couple decades ago, some states kept anti-LGBTQ+ laws on the books. For example, two men named John Geddes Lawrence and Tyron Garner were arrested because of their relationship in Texas. In 2003, the Supreme Court heard their case. The Court struck down the Texas law that prohibited LGBTQ+ behavior. It ruled that people's sexual orientation should be private. "The petitioners are entitled to respect for their private lives," Supreme Court Justice Anthony Kennedy wrote in the decision. "The state cannot demean their existence or control their destiny by making their private sexual conduct a crime."[1] Since the 2015 ruling on same-sex marriage, other laws against homosexuality in the United States have also been struck down.

There's still a long way to go with LGBTQ+ rights in the United States and around the world. People still face discrimination based on their sexuality, such as people who are kept from marrying in certain churches or are denied service by certain businesses. At least 70 countries have national laws criminalizing same-sex relations and nine have national laws criminalizing transgender and gender nonconforming individuals. Some countries even impose the death penalty for homosexual acts, even though it is a personal matter.

Issues of Life and Death

What if protecting a person's privacy means a matter of life or death for themselves or someone else? For example, in some cases, a parent may choose to keep their child from getting medical care. This could be for religious or other private reasons. Many people believe this is morally wrong. They believe that an underage child's right to proper treatment outweighs the parent's right to a private decision about medical care.

U.S. courts have ruled differently on such cases depending on the situation. The courts consider the child's age, the family's reason for declining treatment, and whether the treatment has been shown to work. In 2008, 11-year-old Madeline Neumann died from diabetes complications after her parents refused treatment. The Neumanns were Christian Scientists who believed that prayer alone heals without medical treatment. Even when

Arguments Over Reproductive Choice

Pro-Choice. Pro-Life. The two sides of the abortion argument have been heated for decades. In the 1973 case *Roe v. Wade*, the U.S. Supreme Court ruled that the "right to privacy" (outlined in the Due Process Clause of the 14th Amendment) protects a woman's choice whether or not to have an abortion. Many people believe a woman has a right to decide whether to have a baby. Pro-choice supporters believe this is a personal, private choice that should not be interfered with by the government. They believe that the right to decide belongs to the pregnant woman. Pro-life supporters believe the government should step in to protect an unborn fetus. They believe abortion violates the unborn fetus's right to life, so the government should restrict or ban it. There have been many rallies and protests on both sides of the debate. Pro-life supporters often target Planned Parenthood, a nonprofit organization with health clinics that provide reproductive health care. Though abortions make up only a small percentage of services offered by Planned Parenthood, protests outside clinics are often meant to keep women from choosing abortion.

Around the world, countries hold different views on abortion. It is illegal in all cases in nations such as El Salvador, Nicaragua, the Philippines, and Iraq. In Poland, lawmakers tried to make abortion illegal in all cases. In 2016, women in Poland held large protests stating that it was not the government's decision. The ban on abortion did not become law at that point, but a near-total ban on abortions ended up going into effect in 2021. Some countries, such as Mexico, Indonesia, and Chile, allow abortions to save a mother's life. Others allow abortions in cases of rape or if the baby will not survive. Many western European countries, as well as the United States, protect abortion rights for up to 12 weeks of pregnancy. After that time period, abortion bans and restrictions vary state by state; some restrict insurance coverage of abortion, place bans at specific weeks of pregnancy, or force a pregnant woman to see an ultrasound before her abortion.

their daughter was extremely sick, they would not take her to the hospital. In 2008, a court in Wisconsin convicted the Neumanns of second-degree reckless homicide.

In addition to right-to-life debates around the world, there are right-to-die debates. These discussions concern whether it is a person's private choice to die. In these cases, the person who wants to die is generally experiencing chronic and severe physical pain or a life-threatening illness. The person wants to die with a physician's help, generally through a lethal dose of drugs. This is called physician-assisted euthanasia or suicide.

Some countries recognize the right to die as a private decision. Countries such as Switzerland, the Netherlands, and Belgium allow physician-assisted suicide. Only in Switzerland can a noncitizen obtain a physician's help; because of this, hundreds of people travel to the doctor-assisted suicide clinic Dignitas in Switzerland each year. In the United States, several states allow physician-assisted suicide for terminally ill patients: California, Colorado, Hawaii, Maine, Montana, New Jersey, Oregon, Vermont, and Washington, as well as Washington D.C.

Brittany Maynard was diagnosed with an aggressive brain tumor in January 2014. She was only given a few months to live. She decided that she wanted to have the choice to end her life before cancer did. Maynard moved to Oregon, which has a "Death with Dignity" law. Maynard became an advocate for the right to die. She wrote and spoke on the subject before her death. In November 2014, she decided to end her life, saying, "I've discussed with many experts how I would die from it and it's a terrible, terrible way to die. So being able to choose to go with dignity is less terrifying."[2] Her family went on to continue speaking and advocating for others to have the right to decide when to die.

Some people think allowing physician-assisted suicide would pressure the elderly and sick to end their lives to not be a burden to their families. Some think it is "playing God." Others believe that a person should have the right to decide when they die if they are suffering.

Collecting Private Data

Some concerns over privacy aren't about personal choice—they're about personal records. Governments, in order to run properly, need to keep certain records about people. They need personal records in order to collect taxes, to issue driver's licenses, and to call people for jury duty. Out of respect for privacy, many governments have laws that make sure the records are not accessed by third parties.

Countries such as the United States, Canada, and Australia have privacy acts to protect personal records held by government agencies. The U.S. Privacy Act became law in 1974. The Electronic Privacy Information Center summarized the act:

First, it requires government agencies to show an individual any records kept on him or her. Second, it requires agencies to follow certain principles, called "fair information practices," when gathering and handling personal data. Third, it places restrictions on how agencies can share an individual's data with other people and agencies. Fourth and finally, it lets individuals sue the government for violating its provisions.[3]

Americans' concern over the government gaining access to personal records through third parties was heightened after 9/11, when the U.S. government expanded its powers to more easily view people's records without warrants. The information provided by Edward Snowden in the NSA leak confirmed these fears.

In December 2003, for example, the U.S. government received a tip that al-Qaeda might attack Las Vegas, Nevada. The FBI demanded that businesses there provide all records about tourists who visited over the holiday period. Hotels, car rental agencies, casinos, and more had to turn over purchasing records with people's names, their addresses, their phone numbers, what services they paid for, and what dates they used the services. Allen Lichtenstein, the general counsel for the Nevada chapter of the American Civil Liberties Union, said, "What we seem to be witnessing at this point is a move on the part of the government to keep tabs on what everyone is doing all the time, which has serious civil liberties implications."[4] No known terrorist suspects or associates of suspects turned up in the check.

Some people aren't only worried about the government's ability to collect data; they are concerned about the companies that collect and even sell consumer data. When a consumer buys a product or service, their data is often filed away. Companies can use this data to figure out what the person might want to buy next; then, they advertise that product to them. Many companies, such as social media platforms, have algorithms, or equations, that use user data to decide what the user might be interested in seeing or buying. While companies often argue they only use the data to personalize someone's user and buyer experience, many people have concerns over how their data is used.

Think of the data that people have to give just to shop online: their name, email address, home address, phone numbers, and credit card information. Why is this information sensitive?

A 2019 report from the Pew Research Center found that 79 percent of Americans say they are at least somewhat concerned about how much data is collected about them by companies and 64 percent say the same about data collected by the government. They also found that around 70 percent of Americans feel their personal information isn't as secure as it was five years ago. Few Americans surveyed understood what companies were going to do with their data. Companies get around the legality of collecting and using private data through privacy policies, but many people don't read them—and of the people who do read them, only 22 percent said that they'd read all the way through. That means companies can get away with using data in any way they want, including selling it to third parties. Data breaches are also a big concern; if companies are hacked, people with bad intentions can steal personal data, including credit card and bank information, Social Security numbers, names, addresses, phone numbers, and more. Some laws have been proposed in recent years to regulate data privacy issues, such as the California Consumer Privacy Act (2018), but the

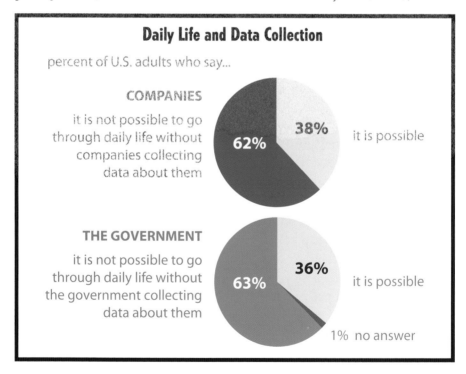

Daily Life and Data Collection

percent of U.S. adults who say...

COMPANIES

it is not possible to go through daily life without companies collecting data about them

62%

38% it is possible

THE GOVERNMENT

it is not possible to go through daily life without the government collecting data about them

63%

36% it is possible

1% no answer

A 2019 survey from the Pew Research Center found that most Americans think it's impossible to go through daily life without the government or companies collecting their data.

United States currently doesn't have a general federal privacy law. The European Union passed its General Data Protection Regulation in 2018, which put power over personal data back into the hands of consumers.

Internet Issues

The government and private companies have more ability to collect and keep data than ever, and a big reason for that is the internet. The internet is everywhere. It is essential for school, work, and communication in the United States and around the world. Because of that, people share a lot of information when using the internet and cell phones, and much of this information is easily traceable. Third parties, such as internet service providers (ISPs) and cell phone companies, store much of this information, and it is easier to sift through electronic data rather than paper records. "Technology makes it easier to keep tabs on millions, even hundreds of millions, of consumers and citizens," wrote David H. Holtzman, the author of *Privacy Lost*. "Not only is the storage of consumers' data cheaper and easier to search than with paper, but also a single person can easily run the whole tracking process."[5]

In the United States, the government has not wanted to restrict the development of new technology. However, this leaves wide-open spaces for information to be misused by governments and companies—with real consequences. The ACLU wrote:

> *With more and more of our lives moving online, these intrusions have devastating implications for our right to privacy. But more than just privacy is threatened when everything we say, everywhere we go, and everyone we associate with are fair game. We have seen that surveillance—whether by governments or corporations—chills free speech and free association, undermines a free media, and threatens the free exercise of religion.*[6]

In 2016, the Federal Communications Commission (FCC) ruled that ISPs could not share or sell personal information, such as location or internet history, without a consumer's permission. This privacy ruling restricted the use of personal data for business purposes. However, in 2017, Congress overturned that rule, so customers' data can now be shared with third parties without their knowledge or consent. Outraged citizens threatened to buy the private histories of Congress members who had voted to overturn

People use their phones for everything—communication, work, shopping, and more. It's important to check privacy and security settings regularly to keep this information safe.

the rule. However, the website The Verge clarified that this would be illegal under the Telecommunications Act, which "explicitly prohibits the sharing of 'individually identifiable' customer information except under very specific circumstances."[7] The law does allow the collection and sharing of aggregate data, which is data collected from multiple sources. Most people still consider this an invasion of privacy because ISPs are able to see a person's entire browsing history. Even though the ISP is not allowed to sell an individual's browsing history to a third party, it is still able to track the websites people visit and use that information themselves to target advertising to consumers.

Without specific laws, ISPs and other companies can decide what information they collect, what they do with that information, and whether they tell consumers they are collecting it. Many companies sell customer data to third parties for marketing purposes. Some of these companies were taken to court for selling the information but not because they broke a federal law; the companies broke their own privacy policies. Additionally, in the United States and other countries, governments may request information from ISPs as well as companies such as Google and Facebook. In the United States, such a request does not necessarily require a warrant. Because of all these issues, some countries are beginning to institute laws that regulate what ISPs, website hosts, and cell phone providers can do with their customer information.

However, where are your internet searches kept, and how can they be used? Online companies keep internet search logs. These logs show what people have searched for online. Companies such as Google can identify which users have visited which websites. People's search and browser histories are not specifically protected by any law.

In 2006, the U.S. government ordered Google to give it a sampling of Google's search logs. When Google refused, the government took Google to court, arguing that it needed the records to show that internet filtering does not protect children from online pornography. The government stated it only wanted random samplings that could not be connected to individual people. Privacy advocates said at the time that this incident was the start of a slippery slope—and it was. By 2014, the Justice Department asked the courts to grant it the ability to remotely access data stored electronically through computer searches. This would be, according to privacy advocates, a major invasion of privacy that could have serious consequences for individuals, even those who have done nothing wrong.

Privacy Rights for Young People

Just because you're not an adult doesn't mean you don't have civil liberties. You also have rights outlined by the U.S. Constitution, such as freedom of speech, religion, and privacy. Sometimes there are specific restrictions on rights for minors, but it's good to know which rights you have.

Reproductive choices are a major privacy issue among teenagers. One issue is whether a teenager can get birth control pills without their parent's permission. In this case, most U.S. state laws protect teens' privacy. They can go to a health professional for birth control; however, some states require teens to get a parent's consent. Abortion is another hot topic. Many states have, or are considering, laws that require parent notification when a teenager decides to get an abortion. Opponents of notification laws believe these laws violate privacy. They also believe these laws force teens to get unsafe abortions. Supporters of notification laws say that parents have a right to know about any sort of medical procedure their teenage children are undergoing.

Confidentiality rights when it comes to minors and their mental health treatment also vary state by state. The American Psychological Association said:

> In some states, for example, a child of a certain age, typically in their early teens, has a right to object to their parent's request to access the minor's record. In other states, the parents are allowed to access the child's mental health records, but there may be limitations—for example, if a court denies access, or the psychologist determines that granting access is detrimental to the minor's psychological well being.[8]

Minors also have some privacy rights in school. The Family Educational Rights and Privacy Act (FERPA) of 1974 protects the confidentiality of student educational records. All public schools as well as private schools that receive federal funding are covered by FERPA. The act gives students and their parents the right to inspect and review their own education records.

Surveillance at Work

Many people use email to communicate and collaborate. The 1986 Electronic Communications Act gives people in the United States some protection from government interference in their email. However, emails have few protections in the workplace, and many Americans are concerned that their employers can read their emails, track their website activity, and more.

Although the U.S. Privacy Act gives them some protection from government interference, most laws do not cover employer surveillance. In fact, many U.S. companies have an electronic monitoring system. Employers can read emails, listen to phone calls, and monitor employee website visits. As more jobs move to work-at-home policies, technology may be used to make sure people are working during work hours, which may involve surveillance. A 2018 survey found that 22 percent of organizations use employee-movement data and 17 percent monitor work-computer-usage data worldwide. Companies are subject to little restriction. If employees use company-owned equipment to conduct personal business, courts have ruled that companies can monitor their use.

The ACLU said:

New technologies are giving employers unprecedented abilities to monitor and watch their workers. Employers have a legitimate interest in monitoring work to ensure efficiency and productivity, but electronic surveillance often goes well beyond proper management concerns and becomes a tool for spying on employees in furtherance of no legitimate business interest. In some cases, employers have even demanded that workers turn over the passwords to their social media accounts.[1]

1. "Employee Surveillance," American Civil Liberties Union, www.aclu.org/issues/privacy-technology/workplace-privacy/employee-surveillance (accessed February 1, 2021).

Some employers—but not all—tell their employees that they are being watched. For now, if people in the United States send emails or check websites at work, they should remember that someone could be watching.

Many schools use dogs that can smell for drugs in lockers.

They can also request corrections and stop the release of personally identifiable information. This law does not protect students from hiding their educational records from their own parents, however.

There are other limits to student privacy. One controversial privacy issue involves searches of students' cars and possessions. In the United States, the Fourth Amendment protects both adults and children and their property from unreasonable searches by the government. Unreasonable searches are those without search warrants. To get a search warrant, law enforcement officials must have probable cause that a crime was committed. It is different, however, in schools. A school official, such as a principal, does not need probable cause to search a backpack or purse. Judges have ruled that school officials have a right to control what occurs at their school.

This also applies to lockers. U.S. courts have found that lockers are shared property between the student and the school, so students should expect minimal privacy with their locker. Drug and alcohol testing at school is another privacy issue. Some students believe testing is an invasion of their privacy. The U.S. Supreme Court has ruled that random drug testing is allowable when students participate in extracurricular activities. In the 1995 case *Vernonia School District v. Acton*, the court said, "Students who voluntarily participate in school athletics have reason to expect intrusions upon normal rights and privileges, including privacy."[9] Learning about your civil rights and limitations as a young person is important. If you think something is unconstitutional, you can speak out about it. That's your right!

Your Opinion Matters!

1. Why is personal choice so important to Americans? Is it important to you?

2. How is the argument about privacy changing as technology changes?

3. What privacy rights do you think young people should have in school?

CIVIL RIGHTS PITFALLS AND PROGRESS

Civil liberties may be guaranteed under the U.S. Constitution, but throughout history and even today, systems and policies have made the nation freer for some than others. These unfair systems and policies often target marginalized groups, such as Black Americans, women, Latinx people, Native peoples, immigrants, LGBTQ+ individuals, and people with disabilities. Protests and demonstrations against such systems and policies sometimes create change and make the nation fairer for everyone. Studying the larger movements for civil liberties and equality can inspire people to keep up the fight for liberty for all. As civil rights leader Martin Luther King Jr. said, "We shall overcome because the arc of the moral universe is long but it bends toward justice."[1]

The American Civil Rights Movement

The history of America is incomplete unless it addresses the role of slavery in building the nation. The 1619 Project from the *New York Times* states: "In August of 1619, a ship appeared on this horizon, near Point Comfort, a coastal port in the English colony of Virginia. It carried more than 20 enslaved Africans, who were sold to the colonists. No aspect of the country

◄ Martin Luther King Jr. is shown here speaking at the March on Washington for Jobs and Freedom on August 28, 1963.

that would be formed here has been untouched by the years of slavery that followed."[2] Until the mid-19th century, many were enslaved by white Americans and did not have any rights at all. In 1865, the 13th Amendment abolished slavery, and formerly enslaved people were recognized as citizens. However, discrimination continued, and segregation laws kept Black Americans from voting and using public facilities in a fair way. Jim Crow laws enforced racial segregation to keep a white supremacist system alive in the post-slavery South.

The civil rights movement of the 1950s and 1960s brought lasting change to the United States. Protests and demonstrations by civil rights leaders, such as Martin Luther King Jr., brought national attention to the injustices faced by Black Americans. It took years of protests and court cases before the U.S government would protect civil liberties for this population. The Civil Rights Act of 1964 outlawed segregation of public facilities and outlawed discrimination based on race, color, national origin, religion, or sex.

In the decades that followed, many peoples' attitudes toward race began to change and the country became more integrated. In 2008 and 2012, U.S. citizens elected Barack Obama, a Black man, to be the country's president. It was a major turning point in American politics, opening the door for many other people of color to hold major roles in U.S. government. In 2021, Kamala Harris became the first Black female vice president and first South Asian vice president of the United States.

Racism Alive Today

The election of Obama did not end the struggles of many Black Americans. About a quarter of Black Americans still live in poverty—nearly three times the rate of white Americans. "A mere election does not change the abject conditions for African Americans or the 230 plus years of racial injustices,"[3] stated Marc Morial, the president and chief executive officer of the National Urban League. Black Americans still face unfair discrimination in educational, economic, and criminal justice systems. One major issue today is racial profiling, which is when a law enforcement officer stops and searches a person because of their color, race, or ethnicity, not because the person has broken any laws.

Between 2011 and 2017, the Stanford Open Policing Project studied nearly 100 million traffic stops across multiple states. They found that officers stop Black drivers more often than white drivers and search the cars of Black drivers more often than white drivers. Critics of law enforcement argue that racial profiling violates people's constitutional rights. The Fourth Amendment guarantees people in the United States the right to be safe from unreasonable searches and seizures without probable cause. Being of a certain race, critics argue, does not give a police officer probable cause. Additionally, critics cite the 14th Amendment. This requires that all citizens be treated equally under the law. Subjecting a person to a search because of their race violates this amendment.

Some state laws allow police to stop pedestrians and ask questions or even search them for weapons or drugs. These laws are called Terry Laws after a Supreme Court case, *Terry v. Ohio*. The Supreme Court ruled in this 1968 case that a police officer could search someone if they had probable cause, which means the police officer must believe a person has committed, is committing, or is about to commit a crime. The Fourth Amendment to the Constitution protects people from illegal searches, but the court ruled that a reasonable suspicion was not a violation of the Fourth Amendment.

New York City called its Terry Laws "stop-and-frisk." The stop-and-frisk program started in the 1990s and resulted in millions of citizens being stopped and searched over the years. Over half a million people were stopped in 2011 alone. Of these stops, 88 percent resulted in no convictions for crimes. Most of the citizens stopped in New York City were Black or Latinx. Many people complained that people of color were unfairly targeted by stop-and-frisk.

On August 12, 2013, U.S. District Court Judge Shira A. Scheindlin ruled the stop-and-frisk program unconstitutional. She upheld the Terry Laws but said the way they were practiced in

Jesse Jackson, a civil rights activist, took part in this 2013 demonstration against stop-and-frisk, which some people argue unfairly targets people of color.

New York City unfairly targeted minorities. She called for the police to overhaul the program under the guidance of an outside lawyer. By 2015, the number of people stopped by New York City police had dropped from half a million to 22,929.

Some people argue that policing grew out of racist systems, and that's why Black Americans are disproportionately affected today. A look back in U.S. history shows that some of the first law enforcement forces in the South were slave patrols, tasked with catching people who ran away from their enslavers. Later, they enforced segregation of free Black Americans. Protests in 2020 over racial profiling and use of force in policing brought international attention to this issue. They started a conversation around how police departments can be held accountable for discrimination and unnecessary force, and how civil liberties can be extended to all people equally, regardless of race.

Affirmative Action and Equal Opportunities

You may have heard the term "affirmative action" come up in debates around race. Affirmative action programs were created to open up schools and workplaces to everyone, regardless of race. For years, employers and schools denied equal opportunities to African Americans and other people of color, such as Latinx people and Native Americans. The programs specifically recruit people from minority groups. Some of the programs give minority applicants preferential treatment.

Preferential treatment makes affirmative action a hot topic. Opponents of affirmative action say it's unfair. They claim that a

Black Lives Matter

The United States faced a wave of protests over police brutality, racism, and racial profiling in 2020. On May 25, 2020, a Black man named George Floyd was brutally killed by a police officer in Minneapolis, Minnesota. Though he was merely suspected of using a counterfeit $20 bill, the police officer knelt on Floyd's neck for nearly nine minutes until he died. Floyd's death was caught on camera, and people watched it around the world, sparking fury. His death called to light many other recent incidents in which Black Americans had been targeted and killed, such as those involving Breonna Taylor (shot by police in her apartment) and Ahmaud Arbery (shot while jogging). This added new energy and importance to the Black Lives Matter movement, which began in 2013 after what many saw as an unjust acquittal (dropping of charges) in the case of the killing of 17-year-old black teenager Trayvon Martin. Black Lives Matter's website says, "Black Lives Matter is an ideological and political intervention in a world where Black lives are systematically and intentionally targeted for demise. It is an affirmation of Black folks' humanity, our contributions to this society, and our resilience in the face of deadly oppression."[1]

By July 2020, the *New York Times* reported that between 15 million and 26 million people in the United States had participated in Black Lives Matter demonstrations. This would suggest that it was the largest movement in American history. Though the overwhelming majority of demonstrations were peaceful, protesters and even journalists were met with great resistance from some police forces, with tear gas, rubber bullets, mass arrests, and militarized gear. It was in stark contrast to the lack of force used against rioters just months later at the U.S. Capitol. Many said this highlighted the difference between how law enforcement treats people of color and white people. Many law enforcement agencies faced pressure to change racist policies and environments and root out white supremacists from their force. Governments also faced calls to "defund the police," or cut their budgets and use the money for community and social services, such as mental health services and youth recreational facilities. Black Lives Matter continues to be a strong movement for change in the United States and around the world; in 2021, it was nominated for the Nobel Peace Prize.

1. "Herstory," Black Lives Matter, www.blacklivesmatter.com/herstory/ (accessed February 1, 2021).

person who is offered a job or admission to a school because of their race is given an unequal advantage. Although some critics do agree that affirmative action was initially needed to get companies and schools to open their doors, they think it is no longer needed because people have equal opportunities. Some white people might feel like immigrants or minorities are "stealing" their jobs, which can inspire white supremacist sentiments or activity. People argue that "diversity quotas" are unconstitutional because it goes against the 1976 Supreme Court case *McDonald v. Santa Fe Trail Transportation Co.*, which prohibits discriminatory preference based on any race, whether minority or majority.

However, many people argue that affirmative action is still needed to correct past wrongs. They also believe that discrimination still happens at companies and schools. Without affirmative action, people of color may lose opportunities. In her dissent after a court ruling on affirmative action in Michigan universities in 2014, Supreme Court Justice Sonia Sotomayor provided support for affirmative action: "The way to stop discrimination on the basis of race is to speak openly and candidly on the subject of race, and to apply the Constitution with eyes open to the unfortunate effects of centuries of racial discrimination."[4] Justice Sotomayor and others agree that affirmative action can help minorities overcome discrimination. Some people say setting diversity "quotas" might be seen as discriminatory, but setting diversity "goals" to hire people from marginalized communities is a good approach to overcoming discrimination.

Harvard Law School was part of an affirmative action lawsuit in 2018 for allegedly staffing their academic journals using race and gender as criteria. These protesters agreed with Harvard's actions to diversify their journals.

Disability Rights Movement

People with disabilities have also been treated poorly throughout history. Common disabilities include autism spectrum disorder, deafness, vision impairment, mental health conditions, intellectual disabilities, and physical disabilities. For hundreds of years, people with disabilities were kept from opportunities, sent away to institutions, abused, and stereotyped. In *City of Cleburne, Texas v. Cleburne Living Ctr.*, U.S. Supreme Court Justice Thurgood Marshall spoke out against facilities for the intellectually disabled, saying, "A regime of state-mandated segregation and degradation soon emerged that in its virulence and bigotry rivaled, and indeed paralleled, the worst excesses of Jim Crow."[5] Until recently, many people with disabilities didn't have the opportunity to go to school or work or access public places. A lack of accommodations in public transportation and public places, such as wheelchair lifts and ramps, kept many people with disabilities from being fully able to participate in society.

While the Civil Rights Act of 1964 outlawed discrimination and segregation pertaining to race, color, sex, or religion, people with disabilities were not included until 1988. In 1990, in an attempt to make things fairer for people with disabilities, Congress passed the Americans with Disabilities Act (ADA). The ADA prohibits disability discrimination in employment, public services, public accommodations, and telecommunications. It was amended in 2008 to broaden the definition of a disability. This means that more people are covered under the law. The ADA is an example of what can be done when a group works together to defend their civil liberties. The ADA passed because more than 100 groups dedicated to disability rights, civil rights, and social justice worked together.

In the years since the ADA was passed, more legislation was created to help people with disabilities gain insurance, education, work, and accessibility, such as the Telecommunications Act of 1996 (which requires telecommunication equipment to be accessible to all) and the Individuals with Disabilities Education Act of 2004 (which ensured free, appropriate public education to children with disabilities). Legislation and public awareness around disabilities can help protect the civil liberties of people with disabilities.

Women's Rights Movements

In the United States and around the world, women have faced discrimination and unequal rights throughout much of history. The women's right movement fought for women to have the right to vote, hold jobs, own property, and earn equal pay.

In 1920, the United States adopted the 19th Amendment, which stated "the right of citizens of the United States to vote shall not be denied or abridged by the United States or by any State on account of sex."[6] In 1972, Title IX, part of the Education Amendments, stated that no one could be excluded from participating in or benefiting from any educational program or activity on the basis of sex. Part of the requirements for Title IX includes protecting students from gender-based harassment and violence, which helps keep women safe in schools and universities. The following year, *Roe v. Wade* ensured women's rights to safe and legal abortions. The past three decades have seen women earning more representation in all levels of U.S. government, from the Supreme Court to the vice presidency. As the late U.S. Supreme Court Justice Ruth Bader Ginsburg said, "Women belong in all places where decisions are being made."[7]

At times, the U.S. women's rights movement left behind an essential part of the population—women of color. Women of color have faced even more discrimination than white women, with more obstacles to gaining representation in government and equal rights. Black men and white women often led civil rights conventions and movements in the past, leaving out Black women. Black women weren't allowed to attend National American Woman Suffrage Association conventions. They still continued to fight for suffrage for both women and Black Americans, forming foundations such as

When they first were allowed in the military, American women were excluded from all combat. However, in 2016, women gained the right to perform any job in the U.S. military, including all forms of combat.

the National Association of Colored Women (1896) and the Alpha Suffrage Club of Chicago (1913). While all white women gained the right vote in 1920, Black women had to wait until the Voting Rights Act of 1965 to fully enjoy this right everywhere in the country. In her victory speech after winning the vice presidency in 2020, Kamala Harris said:

> And so, I'm thinking about [my mom] and about the generations of women—Black women, Asian, White, Latina, Native American women who throughout our nation's history have paved the way for this moment tonight. Women who fought and sacrificed so much for equality, liberty and justice for all, including the Black women, who are often, too often overlooked, but so often prove that they are the backbone of our democracy. All the women who worked to secure and protect the right to vote for over a century: 100 years ago with the 19th Amendment, 55 years ago with the Voting Rights Act and now, in 2020, with a new generation of women in our country who cast their ballots and continued the fight for their fundamental right to vote and be heard.[8]

In many other countries, women have made great strides in their fight for civil liberties and equality. Many countries have adopted laws that allow women to vote and serve in the government. Laws have been instituted that guarantee women equal opportunity in employment and education. In countries such as the United States, those in the European Union, and more, women have the same legal status as men.

Some countries have limited rights for women, seeing them as second-class citizens. Their right to control their own lives is limited by culture and the law. In Saudi Arabia, women need permission from a male relative "guardian" to make basic decisions, such as

Suffragettes such as those shown here fought for women's suffrage, or right to vote.

enrolling in school, getting a passport, or getting married. In Iran, girls can be legally forced to marry at age 13. In both countries, a woman's legal testimony is worth less than a man's, which makes it difficult for a woman to prove that her rights have been violated. In countries where women are seen as inferior, the laws do not protect their basic rights to education, health care, and safety.

In many developing countries, women's property rights are routinely violated. Cultural norms or laws bar women from owning a house or land. In Syria, for example, the government officially protects women's property rights. However, many local communities apply traditional custom rather than the law. They follow the Islamic tradition for inheritance, which grants women only half the share received by men. Many women become impoverished after the death of a husband because they are entitled to such a small portion of his assets.

Governments and groups around the world try to help women in these countries. In the United States, the Office of Global Women's Issues works to advance global women's causes. The office makes sure that women's rights are part of U.S. foreign policy. The United Nations organization UN Women works on economic empowerment, ending violence against women, and giving women a voice in governments around the world.

The LGBTQ+ Rights Movement

LGBTQ+ individuals have been subjected to violations of their civil liberties throughout U.S. and world history. In some countries, it is still illegal to be gay or transgender, and LGBTQ+ people have often been the targets of violence. For instance, in 2017, reports surfaced of human rights violations in Chechnya—gay men were being hunted down and killed, tortured, or held against their will at detention centers. In other countries, LGBTQ+ people have gained more protection of their inherent rights. However, even in these countries, the question of LGBTQ+ rights is hotly debated.

The LGBTQ+ rights movement in the United States began to gain energy in the 1950s with the establishment of the Mattachine Society (the first sustained national gay rights organization) and the

Daughters of Bilitis (the first lesbian rights organization). At the time, gay discrimination was the norm; a 1950 Senate report claimed that gay men shouldn't hold office because homosexuality was believed to be a mental illness. Thousands of gay men and women lost their jobs in the government and military. In 1953, an executive order banned LGBTQ+ people from working for the federal government.

Despite intense discrimination, the U.S. Supreme Court ruled in 1958 that an LGBTQ+ magazine was protected by the First Amendment. Illinois was the first U.S. state to repeal their laws against LGBTQ+ people in 1962, with other states following. In 1969, LGBTQ+ people and police clashed for three days in the Stonewall Riots, which brought national attention to the movement. In the 2015 case *Obergefell v. Hodges*, the Supreme Court ruled that LGBTQ+ couples have the same right as heterosexual couples to be married. Justice Anthony Kennedy gave the ruling. It read in part:

> *It would misunderstand these men and women to say they disrespect the idea of marriage. Their plea is that they do respect it, respect it so deeply that they seek to find its fulfillment for themselves. Their hope is not to be condemned to live in loneliness, excluded from one of civilization's oldest institutions. They ask for equal dignity in the eyes of the law. The Constitution grants them that right.*[9]

As with marriage, gay people argue that denying them the right to adopt children violates their civil liberties. Some state governments agree, but others disagree. In 2008, a Florida circuit court struck down a state law that barred LGBTQ+ people from adopting.

 Within eight years, a judge struck down the last ban on LGBTQ+

When the U.S. Supreme Court declared that same-sex marriage was legal nationwide, the White House was illuminated in rainbow colors to celebrate.

adoption. The state of Mississippi was the last to ban LGBTQ+ people from adopting. The judge cited the ruling that all marriages were now equal after the Supreme Court ruling on same-sex marriage. However, some private adoption organizations still refuse to consider LGBTQ+ people as parents.

Rights for the Undocumented

Should an undocumented immigrant have the same civil rights as a citizen? This is a serious debate today in the United States and abroad. Some people believe health care, education, and basic rights should apply to anyone in a country's jurisdiction. Others believe undocumented people are a drain on the nation's resources and should be sent back to their home country without a trial. These attitudes have led to many attacks on and discrimination against Latinx people, whether they are immigrants or natural-born citizens.

In the United States, many constitutional rights apply to any person on U.S. soil, since the U.S. Constitution often refers to personhood over citizenship. Because of that, they have basic First Amendment rights to speech, religion, press, and protest. They also have a right to "due process of law," including in deportation cases.

Health care for undocumented immigrants is a heated topic. Countries take different viewpoints about this matter. France denies health care to undocumented immigrants. Sweden and the United States federally fund only emergency health care for undocumented immigrants. Even countries with specific policies are not clear about how to deal with every issue. In the United States, all hospitals must treat and stabilize a patient even if they cannot pay. This law means that many undocumented people receive lifesaving treatment. Most of the emergency care given to undocumented immigrants is for childbirth. The Patient Protection and Affordable Care Act of 2010 stated that in order to receive health care outside of an emergency, people must prove their citizenship. This means undocumented immigrants cannot purchase health care or be covered by federal programs such as Medicaid and Medicare. Only U.S. citizens can access this kind of health care.

Another debate is about what the government should provide to children of undocumented immigrants. In 1982, the U.S. Supreme Court struck down a 1975 Texas law that denied free public education to school-age children of undocumented immigrants. Now, children of undocumented immigrants across the country can enroll in public schools. Some immigrants were brought to the United States as minors, and they're often referred to as Dreamers (a reference to the DREAM Act, which has yet to become federal law). In 2012, the Obama administration introduced Deferred Action for Childhood Arrivals (DACA). This kept eligible children of undocumented immigrants from being removed from the United States on a two-year, renewable basis and allowed them to work. While Donald Trump challenged DACA multiple times during his presidency, President Joe Biden committed to keeping DACA and providing a path to citizenship for undocumented immigrants.

What Are Your Rights?

It's important to know what your rights are as a citizen, a minor, and a student, and to understand what people went through to secure basic liberties for Americans as a whole and for marginalized communities. Some people, such as transgender individuals and undocumented immigrants, still have to fight for rights.

Your civil liberties are guaranteed to you under the U.S. Constitution. You may have more rights under your state laws as well. Knowing what your rights are gives you power. For example, if you find something unfair, you can voice your opinion in an acceptable way, even if you're in school. This precedent was set by the 1965 case *Tinker v. Des Moines*; the Supreme Court ruled that students have freedom of speech in school, but that right and others are restricted. Schools have a lot of freedom to decide what statements and actions will interfere with other students' ability to learn.

As the nation's policies change and as technology and attitudes change, the extent of some civil liberties may also change. For example, with the rise of the internet, free speech in schools has become more complicated, and students are sometimes punished for things they post online outside of school hours. Dozens of cases regarding

Immigration and Deportation

Undocumented immigration and deportation were often in the spotlight during the Trump administration. He'd promised a "border wall" as part of his campaign, which he claimed would keep immigrants from crossing into the United States on foot. He sent troops to the U.S.-Mexico border and instituted "zero tolerance" policies that led to deportations, detentions, and thousands of children being taken from their parents indefinitely. There was no plan in place to reunite parents with their children, and many are still in federal custody.

Trump didn't only target immigrants from Central and South America, however. Shortly after taking office in 2017, Trump signed a number of anti-immigration executive orders. Executive orders are orders the president can sign without the approval of Congress that act as laws. In January 2017, President Trump signed an executive order entitled "Protecting the Nation from Foreign Terrorist Entry into the United States." Part of the order included a 90-day restriction preventing citizens of certain countries from entering the country, stating that these foreign citizens would "be detrimental to the interests of the United States."[1] These countries were predominantly Muslim and included Iran, Iraq, Sudan, Yemen, Somalia, and Syria. Many people called it the "Muslim Ban" because Trump's selection of countries seemed quite pointed. Following the 2017 executive order, agents at airports began rejecting citizens of the countries specified in the order. This meant that these men and women were either not allowed to board their plane to the United States or were not allowed through airport security when they arrived

students' right to free speech have gone to court in the last decade and will likely continue to do so in the future.

It's important to study the origins of civil liberties in your country and around the world. Then, you can be an active citizen and participate in discussions around certain rights and their constitutionality. As Founding Father Samuel Adams said, "The liberties of our country, the freedom of our civil constitution, are worth defending against all hazards: And it is our duty to defend them against all attacks."[10]

People across the United States marched against family detention and separation at the U.S.-Mexico border and called to abolish ICE (Immigration and Customs Enforcement).

in the country. The order also suspended the Syrian refugee admissions program even as millions of families and individuals were fleeing a deadly civil war there.

Hawaii's state court declared the ban unconstitutional, but the Supreme Court upheld the ban in 2018. Justice Sonia Sotomayor's dissenting opinion read: "Our Founders honored that core promise by embedding the principle of religious neutrality in the First Amendment. ... Based on the evidence in the record, a reasonable observer would conclude that the Proclamation was motivated by anti-Muslim animus."[2] The ban was erased on Joe Biden's first day as president on January 20, 2021.

1. "Executive Authority to Exclude Aliens: In Brief [January 23, 2017]," Homeland Security Digital Library, January 23, 2017, www.hsdl. org/?abstract&did=798481.

2. Quoted in Nazita Lajevardi, Kassra AR Oskooii, and Loren Collingwood, "Biden Reverses Trump's 'Muslim Ban.' Americans Support the Decision," *Washington Post*, January 27, 2021, www.washingtonpost.com/politics/2021/01/27/biden-reversed-trumps-muslim-ban-americans-support-that-decision/.

Your Opinion Matters!

1. How did the American civil rights movement make America more equal?

2. How can the United States grapple with the pitfalls of its past as it moves into a future that includes civil liberties and equality for all?

3. What do you think are major issues around civil liberties today?

The following are some suggestions for taking what you've just read and applying that information to your everyday life.

- Familiarize yourself with the U.S. Constitution and its Bill of Rights by reading the original text and summaries and analyses from trusted websites.

- Think critically about how the civil liberties outlined in the Constitution and Supreme Court cases might affect you as a young person.

- Educate yourself on current events from trusted, fact-based, and unbiased news sources.

- Research organizations that help protect civil liberties, such as the ACLU.

- Donate to or promote organizations that protect civil liberties.

- If you see civil liberties being threatened in your city, state, or country, bring it to the attention of your elected officials.

- Learn more about civil liberties in other parts of the world and how they are protected, limited, or violated.

- Listen to both sides of debates over civil liberties. Ask yourself, "Why might someone have a different opinion than I do?"

Introduction: The Value of Civil Liberties

1. Quoted in "Franklin Delano Roosevelt Memorial," National Park Service, www.nps.gov/frde/learn/photosmultimedia/quotations.htm (accessed February 1, 2021).

2. Quoted in "John Locke on the Rights to Life, Liberty, and Property of Ourselves and Others (1689)," Online Library of Liberty, oll.libertyfund.org/quotes/497 (accessed February 1, 2021).

Chapter One: Civil Liberties and the American Story

1. U.S. Const. pmbl.

2. Thomas Jefferson, et al, July 4, Copy of Declaration of Independence, July 4, 1776, Manuscript/Mixed Material, www.loc.gov/item/mtjbib000159/.

3. Quoted in "Give Me Liberty or Give Me Death!" Colonial Williamsburg, www.colonialwilliamsburg.org/learn/deep-dives/give-me-liberty-or-give-me-death/ (accessed March 11, 2021).

4. Quoted in "Speech to Virginia Convention," Founders Early Access, rotunda.upress.virginia.edu/founders/default.xqy?keys=-FOEA-print-02-02-02-1924 (accessed March 11, 2021).

5. "The Pledge of Allegiance," Washington Secretary of State, www.sos.wa.gov/flag/pledge.aspx (accessed March 11, 2021).

6. "Do Noncitizens Have Constitutional Rights?," *Slate*, September 27, 2001, www.slate.com/articles/news_and_politics/explainer/2001/09/do_noncitizens_have_constitutional_rights.html.

7. "The Bill of Rights: A Brief History," American Civil Liberties Union, www.aclu.org/crimjustice/gen/10084res20020304.html (accessed January 28, 2021).

8. "The Bill of Rights: A Brief History."

9. "The Universal Declaration of Human Rights," United Nations, December 10, 1948, www.un.org/en/universal-declaration-human-rights/.

Chapter Two: The Importance of Free Speech

1. Robert Shibley, "Cornell's Hostility to Free Speech Hits New Peak," FIRE, September 29, 2008, www.thefire.org/index.php/article/9738.html.

2. Kate Hodal, "Free Speech and Privacy on the Wane Across the World," *The Guardian*, August 8, 2019, www.theguardian.com/global-development/2019/aug/08/free-speech-and-privacy-on-the-wane-across-the-world.

3. Quoted in "Constitution of the People's Republic of China," People's Daily Online, December 4, 1982, en.people.cn/constitution/constitution.html.

4. Quoted in Steven J. Heyman, *Hate Speech and the Constitution, Volume 2* (New York, NY: Garland Publishing, 1996), p. 165.

5. NHCLUAdmin, "Hate Speech on Campus," American Civil Liberties Union, September 4, 2012, www.aclu-nh.org/en/news/hate-speech-campus.

6. "Freedom of Expression in the Arts and Entertainment," ACLU, www.aclu.org/other/freedom-expression-arts-and-entertainment.

7. Quoted in Liberty Hardy, "In Support of Banned Books Week: Quotes on Censorship," *Book Riot*, September 29, 2015, bookriot.com/support-banned-books-week-quotes-censorship/.

8. Quoted in Ashutosh Varsney, "The Political Rushdie," The Journal of the International Institute, Spring/Summer 2003, quod.lib.umich.edu/j/jii/4750978.0010.306/--political-rushdie?rgn=main;view=fulltext.

9. Mike Snider, Roger Yu, and Emily Brown, "What Is Net Neutrality and What Does It Mean for Me?" *USA Today*, February 24, 2015, www.usatoday.com/story/tech/2015/02/24/net-neutrality-what-is-it-guide/23237737/.

Chapter Three: The Right to Religion

1. Javier C. Hernández, "As China Cracks Down on Churches, Christians Declare 'We Will Not Forfeit Our Faith,'" *New York Times*, December 25, 2018, www.nytimes.com/2018/12/25/world/asia/china-christmas-church-crackdown.html.

2. U.S. Const. amend. I.

3. Quoted in "The First Amendment Says Nothing about 'Separation of Church and State' or a 'Wall of Separation Between Church and State.' Where Did This Idea Come From? Is it Really Part of the Law?" Freedom Forum Institute, www.freedomforuminstitute.org/about/faq/

the-first-amendment-says-nothing-about-separation-of-church-and-state-or-a-wall-of-separation-between-church-and-state-where-did-this-idea-come-from-is-it-really/ (accessed February 1, 2021).

4. "Religious Doctrine in the Science Classroom," Anti-Defamation League, www.adl.org/education/resources/tools-and-strategies/religion-in-public-schools/creationism (accessed February 1, 2021).

5. Frank S. Ravitch, "Commentary: Supreme Court Hands Victory to School Voucher Lobby – Will Religious Minorities, Nonbelievers and State Autonomy Lose Out?" *Press Herald*, July 8, 2020, www.pressherald.com/2020/07/08/commentary-supreme-court-hands-victory-to-school-voucher-lobby-will-religious-minorities-nonbelievers-and-state-autonomy-lose-out/.

6. "Religious Displays and the Courts," Pew Forum on Religion and Public Life, June 2007, pewforum.org/docs/?DocID=232.

7. Quoted in Adam Liptak, "Supreme Court Rejects Contraceptives Mandate for Some Corporations," June 30, 2014, www.nytimes.com/2014/07/01/us/hobby-lobby-case-supreme-court-contraception.html.

8. Quoted in Robert Barnes, "Supreme Court Will Not Hear Kim Davis Same-sex Marriage Case," *Washington Post*, October 5, 2020, www.washingtonpost.com/politics/courts_law/supreme-court-kim-davis-same-sex-marriage/2020/10/05/cd5a74d2-0710-11eb-9be6-cf25fb429f1a_story.html.

Chapter Four: Ensuring Safety and Security

1. Paul Burnett, "Red Scare," University of Missouri, Kansas City, Law School, law2.umkc.edu/faculty/projects/ftrials/SaccoV/redscare.html (accessed February 1, 2021).

2. Christopher Finan, *From the Palmer Raids to the Patriot Act* (Boston, MA: Beacon, 2007), p. 142.

3. "H.R.442 - Civil Liberties Act of 1987," U.S. Congress, www.congress.gov/bill/100th-congress/house-bill/442 (accessed February 1, 2021).

4. U.S. Const. amend. II.

5. Quoted in Katie Reilly, "Emma González's Stunning Silence for Parkland: The Latest on March for Our Lives," *TIME*, March 24, 2018, time.com/5213929/march-for-our-lives-live-updates/.

6. Gabrielle Giffords, "Gun Rights Come with Responsibilities," *USA Today*, July 1, 2013, www.usatoday.com/story/opinion/2013/07/01/gabrielle-giffords-gun-rights-column/2480751/.

7. Quoted in Dan Eggen, "Patriot Act Provisions Voided," *Washington Post*, September 27, 2007, www.washingtonpost.com/wp-dyn/content/article/2007/09/26/AR2007092602084.html.

8. Quoted in Anthony Lewis, "The Election and America's Future," *The New York Review of Books*, November 4, 2004, www.nybooks.com/articles/2004/11/04/the-election-and-americas-future/.

9. Saher Khan, "Trump Signed an Executive Order to Keep the Guantanamo Bay Prison Open. Will Anything Change?" PBS NewsHour, February 1, 2018, www.pbs.org/newshour/politics/trump-signed-an-executive-order-to-keep-the-guantanamo-bay-prison-open-will-anything-change.

Chapter Five: Personal Choice and Privacy

1. Quoted in "THE SUPREME COURT; Excerpts From Supreme Court's Decision Striking Down Sodomy Law," *The New York Times*, June 27, 2003, www.nytimes.com/2003/06/27/us/supreme-court-excerpts-supreme-court-s-decision-striking-down-sodomy-law.html.

2. Quoted in Margaret Hartmann, "Brittany Maynard, 'Death With Dignity' Advocate, Ends Her Life," *New York*, November 3, 2014, nymag.com/daily/intelligencer/2014/11/death-with-dignity-backer-brittany-maynard-dies.html.

3. "Privacy Act of 1974," Electronic Privacy Information Center, epic.org/privacy/1974act.

4. Quoted in Rod Smith, "Casinos, Airlines Ordered to Give FBI Information," *Casino City Times*, December 31, 2003, www.casinocitytimes.com/news/article.cfm?contentID=140114.

5. David H. Holtzman, *Privacy Lost* (San Francisco, CA: Josey-Bass, 2006), p. 187.

6. "Internet Privacy," American Civil Liberties Union, www.aclu.org/issues/privacy-technology/internet-privacy (accessed February 1, 2021).

7. Quoted in Russell Brandom, "You Can't Buy Congress' Web History—Stop Trying," The Verge, March 29, 2017, www.theverge.com/2017/3/29/15115382/buy-congress-web-history-gop-fake-internet-privacy.

8. Legal and Regulatory Affairs Staff, "A Matter of Law: Privacy Rights of Minor Patients," American Psychological Association, www.apa-services.org/practice/business/legal/professional/minor-privacy (accessed February 1, 2021).

9. "Vernonia Sch. Dist. 47J v. Acton (94-590), 515 U.S. 646 (1995)," Cornell Law School, Legal Information Institute, www.law.cornell.edu/supct/html/94-590.ZO.html (accessed February 1, 2021).

Chapter Six: Civil Rights Pitfalls and Progress

1. "Dr. Martin Luther King Jr," Smithsonian Institute, www.si.edu/spotlight/mlk?page=4&iframe=true (accessed February 1, 2021).

2. "The 1619 Project," *New York Times*, www.nytimes.com/interactive/2019/08/14/magazine/1619-america-slavery.html (accessed February 1, 2021).

3. Quoted in Stephen Ohlemacher, "Racial Disparities Persist Despite Election of First Black President," *Virginian-Pilot*, November 25, 2008, p. 3.

4. Quoted in Ariane De Vogue, "Justice Sonia Sotomayor: Affirmative Action 'Opened Doors in My Life,'" ABC News, April 22, 2014, abcnews.go.com/blogs/politics/2014/04/justice-sonia-sotomayor-affirmative-action-opened-doors-in-my-life/.

5. Quoted in Derek Warden, "Canonizing Justice Ginsburg's Olmstead Decision: A Disability Rights Tribute," Illinois Law Review, November 23, 2020, illinoislawreview.org/online/canonizing-justice-ginsburgs-olmstead-decision/.

6. U.S. Const. amend. XIX.

7. Quoted in Mary Kate Cary, "Ruth Bader Ginsburg's Experience Shows the Supreme Court Needs More Women," US News, May 20, 2009, www.usnews.com/opinion/blogs/mary-kate-cary/2009/05/20/ruth-bader-ginsburgs-experience-shows-the-supreme-court-needs-more-women.

8. Quoted in *Washington Post* Staff, "Read the transcript of Kamala Harris's victory speech in Wilmington, Del.," *Washington Post*, November 7, 2020, www.washingtonpost.com/politics/2020/11/07/kamala-harris-victory-speech-transcript/.

9. *Obergefell et al. v. Hodges, Director, Ohio Department of Health, et al.*, 556 U.S. (2015), www.supremecourt.gov/opinions/14pdf/14-556_3204.pdf.

10. Quoted in "Popular Quotes," Samuel Adams Heritage Society, www.samuel-adams-heritage.com/quotes/popular.html (accessed February 1, 2021).

FOR MORE INFORMATION

Books: Nonfiction

Karpan, Andrew. *Freedom of the Press*. New York, NY: Greenhaven Publishing, 2020.

Kaul, Jennifer. *The Bill of Rights: Asking Tough Questions*. North Mankato, MN: Capstone Press, 2021.

Levy, Janey. *The Bill of Rights: Guaranteeing Liberty*. New York, NY: Gareth Stevens Publishing, 2021.

New York Times Editorial Staff. *Affirmative Action: Still Necessary or Unfair Advantage?* New York, NY: New York Times Educational Publishing, 2021.

Nichols, Hedreich, and Kelisa Wing. *What Is the Black Lives Matter Movement?* Ann Arbor, MI: Cherry Lake Publishing, 2021.

Books: Fiction

Dimmig, Brenna. *Sanctuary Somewhere*. New York, NY: West 44 Books, 2020.

Johnson, Kim. *This Is My America*. New York, NY: Random House Books for Young Readers, 2020.

Stone, Nic. *Dear Martin*. New York, NY: Simon and Schuster Children, 2017.

Websites

The Constitutional Convention
wethepeople.scholastic.com/grade-4-6/constitutional-convention.html
Learn more about the history behind the
Constitutional Convention.

Jim Crow and *Plessy v. Ferguson*
www.pbs.org/tpt/slavery-by-another-name/themes/jim-crow/
Read about how Jim Crow laws and *Plessy v. Ferguson* restricted the
rights of Black Americans after the American Civil War.

Know Your Rights: Students' Rights
www.aclu.org/know-your-rights/students-rights/
Explore your rights and common questions about civil rights for
young people with the ACLU.

Organizations

American Civil Liberties Union
125 Broad Street, 18th Floor
New York, NY 10004
www.aclu.org
www.instagram.com/aclu_nationwide/
twitter.com/aclu
www.youtube.com/aclu
The American Civil Liberties Union is a national organization committed to defending and preserving the individual rights guaranteed by the U.S. Constitution.

Center for Constitutional Rights
666 Broadway, 7th Floor
New York, NY 10012
www.ccrjustice.org
www.instagram.com/CCRjustice/
twitter.com/theCCR
www.youtube.com/user/CCRmedia
The Center for Constitutional Rights is a nonprofit legal and educational organization that works to uphold the rights guaranteed in the Universal Declaration of Human Rights and the U.S. Constitution.

Lambda Legal
National Headquarters
120 Wall Street, 19th Floor
New York, NY 10005
www.instagram.com/lambdalegal/
www.lambdalegal.org
twitter.com/LambdaLegal
www.youtube.com/user/lambdalegal
Lambda Legal is a nonprofit national organization that advocates for the civil rights of LGBTQ+ people and those with HIV through education, public policy work, and legal cases.

National Association for the Advancement of Colored People (NAACP)
National Headquarters
4805 Mt. Hope Drive
Baltimore, MD 21215
www.instagram.com/naacp/
www.naacp.org
twitter.com/NAACP
www.youtube.com/user/naacpvideos/videos
The NAACP is a U.S. civil rights organization that works toward a more just and equal society, especially for people of color, and to eliminate racial discrimination and hatred.

National Urban League (NUL)
80 Pine Street, 9th Floor
New York, NY 10005
www.instagram.com/naturbanleague/
www.nul.org
twitter.com/naturbanleague
www.youtube.com/user/IAmEmpoweredVideo
The National Urban League is a national civil rights and urban advocacy organization that provides direct opportunities for education and economic empowerment to advance social justice causes.

A

affirmative action, 78, 80
Alien and Sedition Acts, 48
American Academy of Pediatrics, 27
American Booksellers Foundation for Free Expression, 50
American Civil Liberties Union (ACLU), 9, 15–16, 18–19, 24, 26, 37, 45, 53, 69, 72
American civil rights movement, 17, 75–76
American Civil War, 15–16, 24, 49
American LGBTQ+ rights movement, 84
American Medical Association, 27
Americans with Disabilities Act (ADA), 81
Anti-Defamation League, 39
Arbery, Ahmaud, 79
Armed Conflict Location & Event Data Project (ACLED), 26
Articles of Confederation, 13

B

Biden, Joseph R., Jr., 24, 32, 87, 89
Bill of Rights, 6, 13–16, 21, 24, 37, 62
Black Lives Matter, 26, 79
Board of Education, Island Trees School District v. Pico, 30
book banning, 29–30

Boston Tea Party, 12
Brown v. Board of Education of Topeka, 17
Burstyn v. Wilson, 37
Burwell v. Hobby Lobby, 45
Bush, George W., 53, 56, 58

C

California Consumer Privacy Act (2018), 68
Chaplinsky v. New Hampshire, 23
Chbosky, Stephen, 30
Children's Internet Protection Act (CIPA), 31
Civil Rights Act of 1964, 76, 81
Cold War, 50
Communications Decency Act, 31
Constitutional Convention, 13
COVID-19 pandemic, 32, 61
creationism, 19, 39

D

Darwin, Charles, 39
Declaration of Independence, 11–12, 15
Deferred Action for Childhood Arrivals (DACA), 87

E

Education Amendments, 82

Cover LightField Studios/Shutterstock.com; p. 4 Photo 12/ Contributor/Universal Images Group/Getty Images; p. 7 Jana Shea/ Shutterstock.com; p. 8 ANTHONY WALLACE/Contributor/AFP/ Getty Images; p. 10 MPI/Stringer/Archive Photos/Getty Images; p. 12 Stock Montage/Contributor/Archive Photos/Getty Images; p. 13 DNY59/E+/Getty Images; p. 18 (top) Vladimir Cetinski/ iStock/Getty Images Plus/Getty Images; pp. 18 (bottom), 49 Bettmann/Contributor/Bettmann/Getty Images; p. 20 Halfpoint/ Shutterstock.com; p. 25 Thomas Hengge/Shutterstock.com; p. 26 Julian Leshay/Shutterstock.com; p. 29 The Washington Post/ Contributor/The Washington Post/Getty Images; p. 30 LAURENE BECQUART/Contributor/AFP/Getty Images; p. 33 simonkr/E+/Getty Images; p. 34 MikeDotta/Shutterstock.com; p. 38 SAEED KHAN/ Staff/AFP/Getty Images; p. 41 Roberto Machado Noa/Contributor/ LightRocket/Getty Images; p. 44 Bill Clark/Contributor/CQ-Roll Call, Inc./Getty Images; p. 46 Glynnis Jones/Shutterstock.com; p. 50 Eliot Elisofon/Contributor/The LIFE Picture Collection/Getty Images; p. 52 ZUMA Press, Inc./Alamy Stock Photo; p. 53 AFP/ Staff/AFP/Getty Images; p. 54 Jeff Greenberg/Contributor/Universal Images Group/Getty Images; p. 57 Barton Gellman/Contributor/ Getty Images Entertainment/Getty Images; p. 58 Getty Images/ Handout/Getty Images News/Getty Images; p. 59 Halfdark/Getty Images; p. 60 Sipa USA/Alamy Stock Photo; p. 63 dpa picture alliance/Alamy Stock Photo; p. 67 Courtney Hale/E+/Getty Images; p. 70 marchmeena29/iStock/Getty Images Plus/Getty Images; p. 72 alvarez/E+/Getty Images; p. 73 Spencer Weiner/Contributor/Los Angeles Times/Getty Images; p. 74 Mariano Garcia/Alamy Stock Photo; p. 78 Allison Joyce/Stringer/Getty Images News/Getty Images; pp. 80, 85 Bloomberg/Contributor/Bloomberg/Getty Images; p. 82 Jessica McGowan/Stringer/Getty Images News/Getty Images; p. 83 Buyenlarge/Contributor/Archive Photos/Getty Images; p. 89 Antwon McMullen/Shutterstock.com.

Sadie Silva is the author of many books for young people, including a series on the founding documents of America's democracy. She's traveled to many historical American sites, from Jamestown, Virginia, to the Freedom Trail to presidential residences, and hopes to bring the historical ideas of America's Founding Fathers to life for today's young readers.